Let Go

Let Go

A Buddhist Guide to
Breaking Free of Habits

Martine Batchelor

WISDOM PUBLICATIONS • BOSTON

Wisdom Publications
199 Elm Street
Somerville MA 02144 USA
www.wisdompubs.org

Library of Congress Cataloging-in-Publication Data
Batchelor, Martine.
  Let go : a Buddhist guide to breaking free of habits / Martine Batchelor.
    p. cm.
  Includes index.
  ISBN 0-86171-521-7 (pbk. : alk. paper)
  1. Meditation—Buddhism. 2. Habit breaking—Religious aspects—Bud-
dhism. 3. Buddhism—Doctrines. I. Title.
  BQ5612.B36 2007
  294.3'4435—dc22

11 10 09 08 07
5 4 3 2 1

Cover design by Pema Studios. Interior design by Dede Cummings. Set in
Caslon 11.5/15.5.

Wisdom Publications' books are printed on acid-free paper and meet
the guidelines for permanence and durability of the Production
Guidelines for Book Longevity of the Council on Library Resources.

Printed in the United States of America

This book was produced with Environmental Mindfulness. We
have elected to print this title on 50% PCW recycled paper. As a
result, we have saved the following resources: 26 trees, 18 million
BTUs of energy, 2,293 lbs. of greenhouse gases, 9,516 gallons of water,
and 1,222 lbs. of solid waste. For more information, please visit our
website, www.wisdompubs.org

To Lena and Alex who bring me joy and keep changing

Publisher's Acknowledgment

The publisher gratefully acknowledges the generous help of the Hershey Family Foundation in sponsoring the printing of this book.

Contents

CONTENTS

Introduction

Let Go: A Buddhist Guide to Breaking Free of Habits is a book concerned with the transformation of compulsive habits and an exploration of how meditation can support this transformation. As a teacher of meditation for the past twenty years, I have met hundreds of people on courses and retreats, and most people, I have found, are drawn to the practice of Buddhist meditation because they feel blocked somehow or are suffering in some way, in some kind of pain. They hope that meditation will bring them stability and clarity, thus enabling them to deal better with their difficulties. In particular, I have been struck by how much people suffer from persistent habits of behavior that dominate their mental, physical, and emotional lives, and from which they feel powerless to escape. I have been greatly inspired by the changes people have made in understanding and transforming their habitual patterns through applying different kinds of Buddhist meditation.

The meditations described in the book are drawn from different Buddhist traditions. I introduce the practice of mindfulness as a means to focus the mind in order to see clearly what is happening in each moment. This is complemented by the Zen practice of meditative questioning, which helps one understand more deeply what lies at the root of repetitive behavior and what triggers that behavior. Each chapter concludes with an exercise or a guided meditation as a tool for the reader to work with negative habits in a new and creative way.

I start this book by looking at how patterns of behavior emerge through learning and repetition. For example, fear, an emotional pattern that affects us all, can have both positive and negative effects. It ranges from a healthy survival mechanism to a blind reaction that can distort the reality of the situation we face. This leads me to ask: Which are the patterns that we need to change and which are not? And, if they need to be changed, how might we accomplish that? I explain the crucial role meditation has played in transforming some of my own negative and painful habits.

I present meditation as a positive and constructive pattern that has the power to transform our painful habits. One key element of Buddhist meditation is concentration, which helps calm the mind, thereby lessening the power of blind reactivity. Another essential element is inquiry. This helps illuminate the changing nature of experience, thereby unlocking the rigidity that so often results from compulsive habits. When practiced together, concentration and inquiry merge into a nonjudgmental awareness, which enables us to start looking at ourselves and our world in a different way.

By bringing the power of such awareness to our experience, we may discover that *grasping* underlies all negative habits. I point out the dangers of "positive" grasping—as when we strongly desire something—and "negative" grasping—as when we are filled with hatred and rejection. In reducing us to what we desire or hate, both forms of grasping limit the possibility of our responding creatively and freely to the situation. Meditation enables us to experience how grasping happens when the senses are stimulated. By listening in a meditative manner, for example, we can learn to hear even unpleasant sounds in a calm and expansive way. Thus listening can be a point of entry either for negative grasping ("I cannot stand this noise") or for freedom from grasping ("I can creatively engage with this noise").

Mental habits have a tendency to be repetitive, making us feel flat and two-dimensional. In this book, I look at a few such habits, like daydreaming and judging, in detail. I also explore the types of *inner language* we use to describe our experience to ourselves and how it can influence our experience. Awareness helps us to recognize how our habitual patterns of thought have a profound influence on the way we feel. Such habits shape our personality and lock us into fixed forms of behavior. By using questioning meditation we can create a new relationship to our thoughts and thus begin to change the way we think and, subsequently, behave. I look at how Dr. Jeffrey Schwartz used meditation to create a new way to deal with Obsessive-Compulsive Disorder (OCD). I also point out that there seem to be three levels to our mental habits, which I call "intense," "habitual," and "light"—and I propose three separate meditative techniques to deal with these different levels of patterning.

The moment at which a feeling of pleasure or pain begins to turn into a disturbing emotion is the point at which meditative awareness can be most effective. For example, a simple feeling of sadness can easily spiral into a dark and painful emotional state in which we get lost in the "Poor Me" syndrome, convincing ourselves that we are unloved and alone in the world. I explore frequently experienced emotional habits associated with anger, depression, boredom, loneliness, and anxiety. I introduce a practice of meditation on *feeling-tone* (i.e., pleasure, pain, and indifference) as a powerful tool to help us experience our feelings more directly, accept them for what they are, and work with them in such a way that they do not develop into disturbing emotions. I also present the work of John Teasdale, Mark Williams, and Zindel Segal who developed a method called Mindfulness-Based Cognitive Therapy (MBCT) for prevention of relapse in depression.

In addition to mental and emotional habits, we also develop "physical" habits, often as a result of an unskillful or unhealthy relation to the body, such as ignoring or suppressing, due to our tendency to be lost in thoughts and overwhelmed by emotions, the important signals our body may give us. I introduced a practice of body-awareness as a means to give us better access to our sensations. I consider the work of Dr. Jon Kabat-Zinn, whose innovative stress-reduction methods using mindfulness meditation have been found to be highly effective in dealing with physical pain and one's relationship to it.

Next, I explore the question of what we can do when the mental, emotional, and physical habits become so fixed and powerful that they turn into addictive behaviors. Meditation has been found to be a valuable component in a multi-pronged approach to recover from addiction. It is able to provide the vital elements of stability and spirituality. I present how people have successfully combined meditation and the Twelve-Step program, and I suggest that the Buddhist concept of the *ten perfections* could be used as a template to support people who are recovering from addiction.

Our painful habits can also inhibit the potential we have for developing loving relationships with other people. These destructive habits are able to undermine even the feelings we have for our partner, children, family, or friends. By enabling us to see these patterns more clearly, meditation can provide us with the insight and courage needed to transform them. It can also show us how *acceptance* and *trust* lie at the root of love. Moreover, with practice we cultivate greater self-confidence. This makes us less dependent on others for our sense of identity and breaks down the fear that might prevent us from establishing a healthy, trusting relationship. Rather than making us aloof and detached, meditation has an important role to play in issues of intimacy and sexuality.

All life has a social dimension. We are alone but inescapably linked to others in this world. Thus, the question of how we actually treat other people is of utmost importance. Is our behavior driven by deep-seated habits of self-interest? How can we move from a predominantly self-centered relationship with the world to an increasingly *other*-centered one? By reflecting on the fundamental equality we share with others we can feel empathetic identification, which we can then transform into compassionate acts of body and speech, and even mind. In conjunction, meditation and compassionate ethics challenge us to respond to unique and unprecedented situations in a caring and creative way instead of reacting blindly according to our habits.

Finally I consider how we can practice meditation in the hustle and bustle of daily life. I believe that we can dissolve the negative power of our painful habits and transform them, thereby actualizing our potential for wisdom, compassion, and a creative life. In Zen Buddhism, the ten "Ox-herding Pictures" compare the stages on the meditative path with an ox-herder's search for and taming of the unruly ox of the mind. I interpret these images from the perspective of understanding and taming our destructive patterns. Although originating in ancient China, these pictures continue to serve as signposts for a radically new way of living our lives in this world today.

1 Patterns

Repetition and Adaptability

I once saw a four-million-year-old ant inside a piece of amber. It looked exactly like any ant I would find in my garden today. In spite of having had to adapt to changing environments for millions of years, modern ants have remained more or less identical in appearance to that ant in amber. Ants are both extremely resilient and adaptive, which explains why they have been able to survive for so long in almost exactly the same form.

Everything alive has evolved though replication. Repeated patterns in conjunction with occasional mutations are what make the emergence and transformation of life possible. If there were no stable patterns that repeated themselves, it would be impossible for any creature to continue in a consistent form. But were there only repetition and no possibility of variation, the living system would be unable to adapt to change. Thus repeated patterns ensure stability while random mutations allow the possibility of adaptation to new circumstances.

Repetition and adaptability are equally essential for life to continue and evolve.

Robert Wright, in his book *Nonzero: The Logic of Human Destiny*, argues that cultures evolve due to the spreading of information and the development of commerce, enabled by self-interested co-operation. He points out that authoritarianism, which seeks to protect the interests of those in power, often tries to stop change. By suppressing variation, the result is either stagnation or regression, which in the end only breakdown and chaos will change. Likewise, when we too are stuck in a fixed pattern of behavior and resist change, it too can cause us to stagnate or regress. We have a choice. Do we want change to be the result of a chaotic breakdown, or do we want to be a responsible agent, creatively involved in the flux and transformation of our own lives?

Neuroscientists argue that novelty in solving problems is linked to the right hemisphere of the brain, while cognitive routines are linked to the left. Both novelty and familiarity are essential for learning. Learning begins in finding a response to changing situations, which then gives rise to habitual patterns of response once we have been repeatedly exposed to similar situations. As human beings we are constantly moving from novelty to rote behavior.

As a child grows and develops, it is through establishing patterns of behavior that he or she learns how to eat, walk, go to the toilet, read, and write. We are surrounded by patterns; we are made of them and live by them. Some patterns, like eating, are necessary for our survival. Others, like driving a car, are learned activities that make our life easier. Both can simply remain as abilities that we possess or have learned. But they can also develop in positive and negative directions. You can eat wisely and appropriately or greedily and inappropriately. You can be a responsible driver or a dangerous one. What patterns of behavior do you want to cultivate? Are you conscious of how a pattern can start to have a negative effect? And do you want to do something about it?

Afraid of the Dark?

I used to be terrified of the dark. When I was a Buddhist nun in Korea, amenities were basic and the toilets were outside. I was so frightened of going to the toilet at night that I would have heart palpitations from imagining that a man with a knife was going to creep up from behind and attack me. One winter, my companion nuns and I decided to sit in meditation all night without sleeping for five days. I was very worried. How would I manage to go to the toilet throughout the night? So I went to my Zen master, Kusan Sunim, to ask his advice. He told me that whenever I felt afraid, I should return to my object of meditation, which, in the Korean Zen tradition, was the question "What is this?"

I thought the Zen master's question would work as a kind of talisman and thus protect me from any danger. It worked well. My fear vanished when I went to the toilet and I survived the all-night meditation sessions. Some time later, though, it struck me that it was not a magical trick at all. My teacher had given me the gift of paying attention to the present moment. As soon as I came back to the question "What is this?" on my way to the toilet, instead of feeling anxious, I would find myself standing with my feet on the ground, deep in the mountains, in a large monastery in Korea. Who on earth would even know I was there, let alone plan to attack me in the middle of the night?

We often find ourselves in the grip of such emotional patterns, which we then reinforce with habitual patterns of thought. It is entirely natural to be afraid in the dark. It is a good survival mechanism, a valuable adaptive strategy. Because we cannot see well in the dark, our autonomic nervous system is activated and we are primed, ready to move fast at the slightest sign of danger. For a woman walking alone at night in an unknown part of a city, this mechanism is just as important today. But in rural Korea, I would have been far safer at night than during the day, when all sorts of people were coming in and out of the monastery grounds. Some patterns of behavior may be instinctive reactions that no longer make much sense, but once in their grip we still suffer the stress and fear that they provoke.

Who Is Going to Change?

My nephew and my grandmother did not get on at all well. So when the two of them were obliged to stay alone together for four weeks at my mother's house, I was called in to serve as a peacemaker. By the time I arrived, war had been declared and the two of them were not even speaking to each other. Since my grandmother was eighty-five and my nephew twenty-four, I realized that there would be a better chance of getting my nephew to change his ways than my grandmother. I took him aside and asked him why he was so upset with grandma. He said he had trouble with the way she did things—even when they discussed something, he said, they could never see eye to eye.

I asked him if he thought it realistic to expect grandma at her age to change her ways of doing things just to please him. He thought about this for a while, then agreed that, yes, grandma was too old and set in her ways to change. He accepted that the only thing to do was for him to adapt to her and behave differently. A truce was declared and a peace was established that promised to remain in place for the duration of their time together. And I was able to leave with a light heart. A few months later I overheard my nephew explaining to my mother, who was also having troubles with grandma, that she could not really expect her mother to change at her age and she should learn to be more flexible!

If people's patterns are compatible, then they tend to live harmoniously. If they are incompatible, there will tend to be tension and strife. This is one of the reasons that social and cultural patterns develop in the first place. In general, people do not like their patterns to be disrupted. They prefer things to keep happening in a way that is familiar to them. This makes them comfortable, but can also lead to the kind of stagnation and fixity against which a younger generation wants to rebel in order to forge its own identity. Nonetheless, even a rebellious teenager will retain some of her parents' old patterns while at the same time developing new habits and ways of doing things. Over time, old and new come to co-exist and even enrich each other. Again, stability and change are *equally* necessary for a person and a society to evolve and grow. Likewise, when it comes to considering one's own patterns of behavior, some will be found to be perfectly functional, while others might need to be radically transformed.

I often observe the painful effects caused by someone's negative patterns and long for them to see what they are doing and then change. The pain they create for themselves and others seems so self-evident, that one wonders why they persist in saying or doing the same thing again and again. No matter how beneficial it would be for someone to behave differently, entrenched habits are not so easy to overcome. The first problem we face is that it can be very hard for us to see these habits clearly for ourselves. We may be aware of some but remain blind to others until they are pointed out to us.

Blinded by Habits

As a young nun in Korea, one of my responsibilities was to take care of the occasional Western visitors who came to the monastery and answer their questions about Buddhism. Unfortunately, I have always found it difficult to remember all the many lists of terms and doctrines of which Buddhists are often so fond. One afternoon I found myself trying to explain (and remember!) the four noble truths, the most fundamental of all Buddhist lists. I was relieved that I could at least remember the first two: the truth of suffering; that of craving, its origin. But I could not recall the third one—then, just as it was on the tip of my tongue, I noticed from the corner of my eye a monk taking a bucket of persimmons which I had spent most of the afternoon picking. I leapt up, ran over to the monk, wrenched the bucket from his hand and told him in no uncertain terms to whom the persimmons belonged. By the time I returned to our guests, I had remembered the last two truths: that there can be a cessation of craving; and the cultivation of the noble eightfold path.

After the visitors had left, a nun who had been sitting nearby and observed the whole scene asked me if I had noticed anything strange. "Strange?" I said.

"Yes, in your behavior," she replied.

"My behavior?"

"Well, you became very angry with that monk who picked up your bucket of persimmons while you were in the middle of explaining the four noble truths. It was very strange."

Only when she mentioned it did I become aware of what I had done. I had reacted unthinkingly and blindly to the "theft" of "my" persimmons.

A pattern of behavior can become so habitual that one barely notices any more what it prompts one to do. One feels automatically, thinks automatically, and acts automatically. Feelings, thoughts, and bodily sensations are so entangled that it is hard to see clearly which one triggers the automatic behavior. At such times, it may be that all we can know for certain is that we were in the grip of a habitual pattern, which created painful results for oneself and others. We tend to reinforce these patterns by repeatedly thinking and feeling a certain way, and in so doing we come to believe that we have no choice in being the way we are. How often do we think or say in justification of something we have done: "This is just the way I am. I can't help it." But are we really as stuck in our habits as we sometimes assume?

When something unexpected happens, what do we do? Often we are caught in familiar scripts and have a tendency to identify with what they tell us, but this need not be so. Small changes can make an interesting and crucial difference. I recently spent a number of hours correcting a manuscript and then went and deleted all the corrections through misunderstanding an operation of the word processing program. The word "stupid" came to mind. But although it was a stupid thing to have done, that did not mean that I had to agree with the little voice in my head that was telling me what a stupid person I was. Things like this happen because of numerous causes and conditions that come into play at a given time. But it would be a mistake to identify oneself with any one of these circumstances. It is easy and even tempting to say to oneself: "I really am stupid." But as soon as we grasp at something like stupidity and identify ourselves with it, we become fixated on a narrow and incomplete perception of ourselves.

Gripped by Fear

"There is fear in my mind" describes an experience. "I am afraid" starts the process of identification with this experience. "I am a fearful person" goes on to create a solidification of the experience. At different times we may use these phrases as ways of describing much the same experience. But each one registers a discrete perception we have of ourselves and makes us feel differently. The more we repeat them, the more we entrench that perception and feeling.

"What am I afraid of?" "Where does the fear come from?" "Who is afraid?" As long as we can ask these questions, we keep open the possibility of looking at the origin and conditions of the fear, perceiving things otherwise and diminishing the identification and the solidification. We can live more lightly with ourselves and thus be less stuck in a fixed view of who we are. As soon as we have convinced ourselves that we are a fearful person by nature, we are stuck. Then even the most trifling thing can make us afraid. It seems that fear is our natural state.

Every few years I go to South Africa to teach meditation. Through pictures and stories in the media, one could easily have the impression that this is a very dangerous place. And indeed, for some people living in certain places it is. But on all of my trips, which have taken me extensively throughout the land, I have never once been hurt or in any danger at all. Nonetheless, I have felt deeply afraid in South Africa. Why?

After a while I realized that what made me afraid was not the presence of any real danger, but *other people's fears*. Whenever I found myself with South Africans who were nervous and afraid, then I would start being nervous and afraid too. It was a contagious pattern of feeling. But if I was with strong, optimistic people who had fought hard to overthrow the apartheid system, I would experience no fear at all. Since then I have aspired to such fearlessness that can be transmitted to others. What greater gift can there be than to give peace of mind to oneself and others?

South Africa is an excellent place to work with fear. As long as I cover myself well and do not wear or carry anything ostentatious or expensive, I can be assured I have done my duty to my survival instincts. Then I can start enjoying life as it comes. I learn a great deal from visiting social projects in townships or meeting people in their smoky village huts. I can encounter them as individuals leading their own lives, suffering and rejoicing just as I do. A threatening, one-dimensional image of them is banished from my mind. They are simply human beings like myself, trying to live a full and true human life within difficult circumstances.

I sometimes go into a men's prison near Cape Town to lead a meditation class for inmates, most of whom have murdered someone or committed a violent crime. But they have learned how to meditate and practice diligently. Meditation helps them to see their destructive patterns clearly and to understand what led them to being where they are now. Many of them see their time in prison as an opportunity to transform themselves. They might appear to be stuck in a jail, but they do not need to feel stuck in their minds.

EXERCISE
Becoming Aware of Habits

Sitting on a chair at a desk or a table with a piece of paper and a pen, try to become aware of some of your habits in a nonjudgmental way. Before we transform our habits we have to *see* them clearly, in a nonreactive way. We are not bad people because we have certain habits—just human. Certain habits are beautiful and useful, other are painful and destructive. And most of us have some inkling of them. People we know or who are close to us might have pointed some of them out to us already!

This exercise is an invitation just to be open and present to a few patterns. It does not have to be exhaustive. We just want to be aware of some of them gently, kindly, and with a little humor, if at all possible.

Write down the name of two of your *positive* patterns, like kindness and attentiveness. It is as important to be able to see our positive habits as our negative ones.

Describe one negative habit, maybe some tendency toward irritation or fearfulness. Try to be an impartial and kind witness. Try to see the fact that you do not *always* act from that habit, and like all habits, this one arises out of certain circumstances.

As you sit still in silence, are you aware of a habitual thought—a common and recurring thought or storyline? Just be conscious of thoughts that are relatively repetitive. Try to be like an inquisitive explorer with a fresh and open mind.

Feeling in the region of the solar plexus, are you aware of a certain habitual feeling? Do you habitually feel joyful, peaceful, sad, irritable, or relatively okay? Even habitual feeling will be changing, coming and going.

What do you feel in the body?

Are there any habitual sensations? Do you experience certain regular discomfort in the middle of or after certain situations? What is it that alleviates it? Try not to identify with or solidify the sensation. Try to breathe through it.

Complete the exercise by standing up and going about your daily activities. As you go through your day, try to notice gently and kindly the habitual thoughts, feelings, and sensations that you experience. It is important to see this exercise as an objective but friendly observation. You are not looking for a culprit, you are just trying to understand and know the conditions in which you find yourself.

2 Meditation

The Four Great Efforts

Many of the teachings in this book draw on the teachings and traditions of Buddhism. The Buddha encouraged his followers to make four great efforts:

to prevent from arising negative states that have not arisen
to let go of negative states once they have arisen
to give rise to positive states that have not yet arisen
to sustain positive states once they have arisen

These efforts encourage the cultivation of positive patterns as a means to help overcome negative patterns. But although they are *simple*, they are by no means *easy*.

It is not just a question of banishing what is negative and affirming what is positive. The Buddha suggests that over time we consciously create the conditions that *prevent* negative thoughts and emotions from occurring in the first place as well as the conditions that naturally enable positive thoughts and emotions to occur. The teachings of Buddhism emphasize how everything in life is the consequence of causes and conditions, and these four great efforts are meant to help us develop the causes and conditions for more peace, stability, joy, and openness.

Beneath the surface of our consciousness lie numerous mental and emotional patterns that, when certain conditions arise, prompt us to behave in a destructive, self-defeating manner. These patterns are easily triggered and once triggered take us to those same familiar but painful places. Yet, if we spend time cultivating constructive and positive responses in their place, we will discover that they have the capacity not only to weaken the power of our negative patterns but even to disable the trigger mechanisms that spark them. Much of Buddhist meditation consists of a systematic cultivation of positive patterns that enable us to engage creatively with those negative patterns that cause us pain.

Concentration

There are two vital elements in Buddhist meditation: *concentration* and *inquiry*. *Concentration* is the ability to remain focused for a sustained period of time on an object. Some teachers will suggest a total one-pointed concentration on a single object. Personally I would recommend to be focused on one *type* of object in one's own experience but within a wide-open awareness in the background, in order to develop an inclusive type of concentration, which is stable and open at the same time. Concentration leads to calmness and stillness of body and mind. *Inquiry* is the ability of the mind to notice clearly what is happening and look deeply into its nature. It, in turn, leads to insight and wisdom.

There are four traditional positions in which you can

meditate: sitting, standing, walking, and lying down. If you can meditate sitting up, you need to sit in an upright and relaxed posture. You become aware of your body sitting on the chair, your buttocks on the cushion, your feet on the floor. If you need to lie down to meditate, lie comfortably on your back and become aware of your body as it is lying down on the bed or floor.

Know that you are safe; nothing else is happening; you are breathing and alive.

Then focus on the breathing, gently letting your attention come to rest on the natural rhythm of inhaling and exhaling. In this way, the breath acts as an anchor to the present moment. At the same time, you are also conscious of the sounds, feelings, sensations, and thoughts in the background of your awareness. The meditation does not exclude any-thing. Focusing on the breath in the context of a wide open awareness grounds you in the present moment, preventing you from rushing and jumping ahead or scattering yourselves in all directions. In the foreground you are focusing on the breath, in the background various things arise and pass away.

Before long, feelings or thoughts, which seem more com-pelling than the breath, are likely to intrude and demand attention: something a colleague said or did at work, plans for later in the day, a worry or a memory. We spend a great deal of time lost in and enslaved to such thoughts. It is both revealing and restful just to let them be and not pursue them by simply returning to the breath whenever they distract us. If we get lost or diverted again, then once more we come back to the breath. What could be more essential and primordial than just resting with the breath, the very ground of our life?

If we do this kind of exercise regularly, it enables us to cul-tivate stillness, spaciousness, and openness. It is simple but effective. As long as we are focusing on the breath we do not

feed our mental, emotional, and physical patterns. By returning to the breath again and again we start to dissolve their
power. We develop a space between experience and our identification with it, thereby weakening the process that creates
habits in the first place.

In meditation we do not flee from any experience, but learn
to experience our self and the world more spaciously.

Inquiry

The second vital element of meditation is inquiry. This is the
ability to question vividly what is happening. It is like a beam
of light that illuminates the fluid, changing, and conditioned
nature of experience. A common pattern of the human mind
is to be locked into a rigid and fixed view of ourselves and the
world. Meditative inquiry enables us to look deeply into what
is happening in each moment and see its changing and condi-
tional nature. We come to understand the extent to which we
are blind to such features of our existence and instead remain
caught in repetitive emotional and mental habits that are built
on the illusion that we never change.

One of my patterns is to become easily irritated and react
angrily. Meditative inquiry helped me to see this habit
directly and experientially as it took place in my own body
and mind. I realized that it was fruitless merely to wish it away
and painful to lose myself in this angry emotion.

I once had a heated argument with a friend about preparing
some rooms in our community for guests. But we had to cut
the discussion short as I had to go and cook. As I was preparing the meal, I suddenly noticed how angry I was and began
to inquire into what was going on. My heart was hammering
and my arms and legs were shaking. I realized that nobody else
was causing me this pain but myself. I alone was the creator of

this suffering. As soon as I realized this, my body calmed down and I relaxed. Then I looked into the thoughts that were still racing around in my mind. I kept repeating to myself: "Yes, I am right. She is wrong." And I recognized then that my friend was probably thinking exactly the same thing. As soon as I saw the absurdity of this pattern of thinking, it began to stop.

It took me some time to be able to see this. First I had to see and accept this pattern of irritability. Then I had to uncover its causes and conditions. Then by diving directly into it, finally its power could be dissolved. But even by just seeing and accepting, we will shorten the length of time these patterns will last. By knowing the causes and conditions, we will further lessen their power.

In the light of awareness, finally I understood the futility of identifying with, and thus defining myself by, these phrases in my head. In the midst of an argument, it is very easy to over-identify with our opinion of that moment. When someone challenges that opinion, it feels as though they are challenging us, rather than an idea in our head, which, in the end, is nothing more than the firing of neurons. Do we really want to reduce ourselves to the firing of a few cells in our brain?

We are far more than that at any moment. We have a tendency to identify with our ideas. But ideas are just a small part of what our brains are capable of thinking of. Moreover we change ideas again and again. It seems too limiting to define ourselves with just *one* idea. We can have so many different ideas. By locking onto one like "I am right," which can lead to "I am always right," we stop ourselves from opening to the ideas others have and from having a fruitful dialogue with them, when their ideas could enrich our own.

Acceptance

Cultivating concentration and inquiry together enables us to develop a meditative awareness, which is characterized by *acceptance*. This acceptance is borne of knowing ourselves in a stable and open manner. We see directly and experientially what is there and embrace it fully. This acceptance leads to a creative engagement with what is happening within and outside ourselves. It allows the possibility of meeting ourselves in a different way. The space, calm, and openness of such awareness all help us to stop identifying with any one particular aspect of our experience. Instead of judging what is happening, we can assume an interest in what is taking place.

Often we are quick to judge ourselves and others, but by identifying with the judgment, we reduce our field of awareness and thus of action. "I am like this. They are like that"— such affirmation stops us from fully engaging with the totality of our experience. Concentration helps us to look directly at the experience with stability. Inquiry brightens the possibilities in the moment. Moreover acceptance makes us say "Yes, I see that I am acting in a certain way, but where does this come from? How has this action, feeling, or sensation arisen? What is the impact of my actions on others?"

Far from being self-obsession, this is an encounter with the totality of our experience. Self-obsession would make us self-referential, bringing everything back to our own person. Meditative acceptance enables our awareness to radiate out and allows us to see ourselves in a wider context and not just be defined by our own existence and needs. This in turn lets us be interested and concerned with the existence of others and our impact on them. The awareness and the acceptance developed in meditation is not only awareness and acceptance of ourselves but also awareness and acceptance of others.

Moreover, this kind of practice can help you see more clearly and accept what is good, skillful, and kind within you: your positive patterning. In order for this goodness to become alive and activated, you need to recognize it, feel it, and affirm it. The Buddha said that goodness needs to be to fed and nurtured for it to be able to develop further.

In my youth I wanted to become a journalist, but I never thought I would become a writer since I always had such bad marks in writing and composition at school. But my translating of Zen Master Kusan Sunim's lectures led to their publication, which in turn led to co-editing a book on Buddhism and ecology, which finally resulted in my starting to write myself. If I had initially wholly identified with the perception of myself as a bad writer, I doubt I would have responded positively to suggestions that I edit and write.

If you lock yourself into repetitive patterns, it is difficult to evolve. You are convinced that there is no way for you to be different. But if you allow yourself the possibility of change, you thereby plant a seed, which, if cultivated, might lead to unexpected and remarkable developments. A seed is tiny, but when it is planted, watered, and cared for, a great tree can be born. If not planted, the seed will simply remain as it is. This is the process of life and of evolution.

When our minds are rigid and fixed, our horizons become limited. We close in on ourselves; nobody and nothing can reach us. This is real self-absorption, the opposite of meditation. Our patterns are often developed as a means of survival when we are young, when we are helpless and not in charge of our destiny. Such patterns—extreme carefulness, being too judgmental, or escaping from problems by daydreaming—are often essential in helping us to survive and keep our head above water. We may no longer need these coping mechanisms when we become adults, but having become so used to them, they are now nonetheless established as deeply ingrained habits. I have a friend who had a brutal childhood. Her way to cope was to space out. Now as an adult she has a quiet and peaceful life but she finds it quite difficult to stay in the present although it is happy and nonthreatening. In fact, these habits might start having the *opposite* effect than they did in childhood. They become obstacles, they get in the way of our doing other things, they keep leading to painful outcomes, but we seem unable to stop them. They are too familiar to us. We are frightened of trying to do something that we have never dared do before.

The Power of Awareness

A regular practice of meditation is a good way to develop the power of awareness, a power that can eventually become stronger than the power of your negative habits. The power of awareness gives you the strength to do things differently and the courage to go beyond your habitual limitations.

For many years I suffered from a strong pattern of rejection if someone hurt me. I would not talk to him or look at her for days. One day I saw the pattern as it started to arise. I saw clearly that I was about to close off to someone. At that moment, the power of awareness was strong enough to stop me and offer me a different way of responding. I was still terrified by the unknown into which I was about to enter, but I chose to go beyond the fear, to smile and reach out to the other person instead of closing off. I was surprised by the ease in my heart that this produced. It felt so peaceful. What truly shocked me was the sudden realization of how painful it must have been for the people I had rejected in the past.

Cultivating concentration and inquiry enables you to see your habits more clearly. At first, you may not notice a pattern until it has already repeated itself. Someone does something you dislike; you react in a habitual way and are quickly taken over by the power of the pattern. After a while, when the reaction has played itself out, you sheepishly realize that once more you have let yourself be caught. But over time, you notice the habit more quickly and are even able to take an interest in it. There is a stage at which, when you catch the pattern in the middle of its cycle, you are aware of being caught in a familiar place—but you are still unable to counter the force of your habitual feelings or thoughts. This is the most difficult stage. You know it is painful and unskillful to behave in such a way, but you cannot help yourself. Over time, the duration and the intensity of the habit will become less simply as a result of your being more aware of it.

Meditative inquiry helps us recognize the words, feelings, or conditions that trigger our reactive habits. This clear, focused attention is what allows us to catch ourselves at the *beginning* of the cycle. We remember and reflect on the four great efforts. We come back to our breath and body in this moment. We inquire into the situation and try to open our heart to the people involved. After doing that, we can also look for ways to help us create movement and space so we can move away from the automatic reaction. We may go for a walk, phone someone, read, write, or dance. This weakens the power of the trigger and the alchemy that ignite the habit and we start on the path to freedom. Finally, we can see the pattern before it arises and find the freedom to choose another course of action. Then our heart opens and our mind clears. What we had not dared hope for has been made possible.

EXERCISE
Meditation on the Breath

Sit still in a relaxed posture with the back upright on a chair or on a cushion on the floor, with the eyes half-closed, not fixing anything.

How does it feel to be breathing? Try to experience your breath consciously.

Rest your attention gently on the in-breath and the out-breath.

Feel the air coming in a little cooler. Feel the air coming out a little warmer.

Wait for the breath to happen and follow it as it comes and goes.

When habitual thoughts about plans for the day come up, gently and steadily come back to the breath, remembering your intention to be aware and awake in this moment.

When habitual feelings of uneasiness arise, let them pass through you while you rest your whole being on the breath.

If you experience a certain discomfort in the back, try to be aware of it openly without identification, and see it rise and pass away as you try to focus on the breath.

Whenever you come back to the breath, you come back to a full awareness of the moment.

Being one with the breath, you are one with life and the world.

At the end of the meditation, open the eyes fully and feel your whole body sitting upright.

Then consciously stand up and try to bring the awareness you developed during the meditation to everything you do and every person you meet during the day.

3 Grasping

No-thought is to see and to know all things with a mind
free from grasping. When in use it pervades everywhere,
and yet it sticks nowhere.

THE SIXTH ZEN PATRIARCH, HUINENG

To Stick or Not to Stick?

Grasping is a primordial pattern. We often feel that the world is sticky or that we are somehow *adhesive*—things stick to us. Each time we come into contact with an object through our senses—visual objects, sounds, smells, tastes, sensations, or thoughts, the pattern of grasping has an opportunity to manifest. For example, as soon as we look at something, we identify with it: "I" am seeing a flower becomes quickly "I" like this flower, "I" want this flower for "myself." As an experience, it is not impersonal, we do not comment inwardly: "there" is a flower, the flower exists, or the flower is perceived. If "I" have a thought, I do not experience or say to myself, "there is a thought." Rather, it is immediately "my" fantastic thought or "my" terrible thought. A problem instantly becomes "my" problem and the only thing that exists in my life at this moment.

When we are not grasping, our experience can become more vast and we can creatively engage with the world in an open manner. In this way, we begin to *purify* the mind. This kind of purification doesn't have anything to do with becoming perfect and saintly, or even getting rid of all *im*purities. This kind of purifying the mind means coming into contact with the world without holding on and to encounter events and conditions fully without being attached to or disturbed by them.

By identifying with what we perceive and experience, we solidify ourselves and the object of perception. By solidifying ourselves we reduce ourselves to what we grasp at. By reducing ourselves to what we grasp at, we magnify it and then we become truly stuck, and we will feel paralyzed and not free. The thought has me instead of my giving rise to a thought that is ephemeral and rising upon certain conditions. By doing this we exaggerate a thought's power.

This mechanism can be shown by way of a practical example. I hold something dear, a small Korean golden bowl, for example. Because it is mine and it is precious, I grasp at it. So physically I hold it in the palm of my hand and tighten my fist around it. If I do this for some time, I will get a cramp in the arms. But also I will not be able to use my hand for anything else, which means that I am *stuck to* what I am grasping at. The solution to the grasping pattern upon contact is not, of course, to get rid of the hand that grasps or to get rid of the object being grasped at. That is too drastic. The object has not asked to be grasped at, even if advertising and packaging made it incredibly alluring. Meditation can help me open my hand gently and have the object rest lightly upon my palm; in this way there is the possibility of movement and freedom.

Negative Grasping

We grasp in two ways: by wanting and by rejecting. When we reject something, we are grasping at it in reverse and the same process of identification, solidification, isolation, limitation, and magnification happen. Remember the last time you hated someone. You could not stand to see that person. If you happened to see him, you noticed immediately all his flaws and he was constantly on your mind. When we grasp in rejection, we tighten around an object or a person and expend a lot of energy around that object or person. This could explain some of the tension and exhaustion in our life.

Several years ago, I went on a month-long silent retreat in a new meditation center in North America. As is usual on such a retreat, I had a daily job, which I did for one hour a day. Since I like cutting vegetables, I chose to work at 8AM to prepare vegetables for lunch, our main meal of the day. We were thirty retreatants, so there were a lot of vegetables to chop.

I have a weak stomach and cannot eat bell peppers of any kind—yet our cooks seemed to have a certain fondness for that particular vegetable and every day I was greeted by the sight of a pile of peppers to chop. So I knew there was at least one main dish I would not be able to eat at lunch. Since this was a daily event I had opportunities to get upset on a regular basis. I could see that I had the choice of grasping at the peppers or not, to identify as them being an obstacle to my meditation or not.

One afternoon I was looking at wispy clouds racing through space. At that moment, I saw that the peppers could be like the clouds passing through the sky. I could let them move though my field of vision, and so encounter their sight in a spacious way, or I could be like a hedgehog; anything that falls on its back would get stuck onto its quills and rot away. In this instance, concentration enabled me to create space when coming into contact with the peppers, and inquiry helped me to see the negative consequences of grasping at them so I could deal with them in a lighter way.

When I returned to Europe from Korea and lived in England I became a house-cleaner for ten years. One of my most dreaded moments was when cleaning bathrooms, especially the toilets. What would I find in the toilet bowl? I would recoil with great distaste if I found anything and would flush it fast while looking away. Then one day while doing a community meditation retreat I went to do my cleaning job as usual. I entered the bathroom very calmly, lifted the toilet seat, and there was something big and brown floating there. I was not upset. I observed it carefully with interest and impartiality, and saw that it was just matter—nothing more, nothing less. I still flushed it because it was not supposed to be there for very long and it was my job to clear it away. There was no disturbance—just openness and clarity—because in that moment there was no exaggeration. The meditation had created the space to see the thing differently.

The problem is not with any thing itself but with the *exaggeration* of its badness. This I could clearly see when my grandmother was ill and incontinent. I was taking care of her on my own for a few days and one morning she had managed to drip feces on the carpet of her bedroom. Coming to get her up I did not see it and walked in it and trailed it everywhere until I saw what she had done and I had done. For a moment I was paralyzed and I started to feel the habitual tremors of panic, anger, and helplessness when faced with an unexpected and difficult situation. But I realized they were unnecessary. I did not need them and they would not help me deal better with the situation. On the contrary, they would kill wisdom and compassion.

So I did not exaggerate the sights that faced me and decided to take care of the situation as it was. I saw that even this situation could be accommodated and dealt with skillfully and compassionately. The only thing needed was to clean one spot at a time—first grandma, then the bedroom, then the dining room, then the kitchen. I was surprised that I could achieve this in an hour without undue hurry. I understood then that if I did not grasp nor exaggerate, I could be more efficient and at ease.

Encountering the World of the Senses

Our encounter with the world is multidimensional. We see a flower, we recognize it as a flower, we see its colors, we feel the texture of its petals, and we can smell its perfume.

Yet when we see something, can we really see it, encounter it, and respond to it in a non-grasping nor exaggerating manner? If we *identify* with it in any way, the process of grasping will ensue; solidification will be followed by limitation, magnification, and exaggeration.

If I see a pretty but expensive dress in a shop window, do I see it as the dress of the season that "I" must absolutely have to feel better about myself and impress all my friends? Or do I see a pretty dress with nice colors and shape that possibly I could try on at some point if I have the money and the time to check on it? In the first situation there will be much aggravation, thoughts, and feelings about getting the dress. In the other, there will be lightness and openness as the object is not encountered in such a tight and obsessive way because my identity does not rest on buying and possessing it.

I used to visit regularly two Zen masters in Korea when I was a Zen nun. What was noticeable about their presence was the absence of tension. They felt very spacious. Often if I had something bothering me, it would evaporate when I visited them. It was as if their spaciousness and openness, their "non-graspingness" was contagious. Sometimes we feel this way ourselves, when we do not grasp at anything and our heart opens, we can creatively encounter and engage fully with that moment.

Seeing

I came back to Korea in 2004 after many years away. Everything had changed, huge apartment blocks had sprouted up everywhere, even at the base of the small temple belonging to a monk friend in the suburbs of Seoul. This temple used to be in the countryside surrounded by hills and pine trees. The green hills are still there at the back but in front the only view is of these huge buildings ten times bigger than the temple. I wondered how my friend could live there.

Yet it would be fruitless and painful to hate the apartment blocks because, after all, they will never move away. Instead he just sees them as they are, big and tall with a lot of people who need a place to live and who also have Buddha nature, the potential to awaken. Meditation enables us to look beyond the simple immediate contact of things to the conditions that gave rise to them. It helps our contact with the world become richer and more multifaceted.

During my retreat in Massachusetts, every day I would go for long meditative walks on the snowy paths. In the forest there were birch trees growing here and there. I loved these trees: they were so tall, straight, and white. I would stare at them standing in the snow. For a while I could commune with their beauty with no agitation in the mind and then I would start to grasp and proliferate. "Hmm, I really like those trees. It would be nice to have such trees in my back garden. Yes, hmm, the garden should be big enough. Where could I find those trees? What about that garden center near Bordeaux?" By then I was not with the tree anymore, I was in France and in the future. None of this is to say that we cannot appreciate beauty, only that real appreciation will disappear as soon as we grasp and plan, as grasping and planning will remove us from the experience of beauty itself.

Another thing that we do in terms of visual objects is to visually grasp at something that is not there. This is especially pernicious. In 2000 my husband and I moved from England to live in France. Our house was in the process of renovation. We converted the attic into my husband's office and a small meditation room but we needed a staircase to reach these rooms. I had the vision of a beautiful staircase in hard wood. However it was difficult to get a good carpenter, and in desperation we asked the only carpenter we could find to make it. We did not get the dreamed-of staircase. Instead we had to settle for something very functional, in pine with steep steps.

Whenever I used it, there was a feeling of discrepancy and distaste—until I paid close attention. I started to notice that when I trod on it I was actually seeing *two* staircases next to each other—the one that was there and the other imagined one that wasn't. I did not encounter the staircase as it was but as it should have been. The frustration was totally self-created and unnecessary. As soon as I saw that I was grasping at something that was not there, I let go and then could use the humble staircase peacefully. After all, it did the job well enough.

Notice if you grasp in this way at anything that is not there. Do you go around with a double vision of things—what is and what you would like to be or what is not there? It's a painful way to live as it creates in your life an undercurrent of frustration.

Grasping

Often one of the things we may grasp at is the way we look. Often in our mind we have a certain idea of how we look and we are surprised when we look at ourselves in the mirror when the image in the mirror does not correspond to the mental image. It can even become dangerous to grasp at that mental image. One form of anorexia seems to come from a serious aggravation of this type of double-vision grasping. The anorexic person has a wrong body perception due to mal-adaptation such that what they see in the mirror does not correspond to the mental image of their body created in their brain. To match the two body images, they have to starve themselves. An extreme example, but it's so easy for many of us to do versions of this.

Listening

One of the constant stresses of modern life is noise: ambient noise, street noises, the noise of other people's lives.

When we moved to France, there was a large concrete foundation in the garden that we wanted to remove, but it was extremely thick and a man had to come to break it up with a pneumatic drill. The day the worker came with the drill was beautiful and I wanted to work in the garden right next to him. But the sound was very powerful, almost overwhelming—so I decided to experiment with *listening meditation*.

In listening meditation, you listen to sounds without analyzing, naming, grasping, or rejecting any noise that might occur. You do not go following after sounds, but instead you let them come to you. You focus on them as they arise with wide-open awareness.

This is what I proceeded to do in the garden. As I dug the bulbs out, I went into the sounds produced by the pneumatic drill. It was very powerful and all-encompassing sound, but it wasn't just a single noise. When I really paid attention, listened *intently*, I could also hear it was fluid and changing. I noticed that when I went away to plant the bulbs, I seemed to have *more* opportunity to be bothered and grasp at the ear-shattering noises. When I came back close to them and went completely into the sound, I was totally fine. The focused attention enabled me to experience the noise in a *spacious* way. But as soon as I created a separation from the sounds and felt myself apart from them, judgment and dislike arose. I could see clearly that I had a choice—to create space within hearing this sound or fix myself and the sounds, as two separate entities not flowing in a continuum of contact and relationship, thereby giving rise to tightness and tension.

Once I was teaching meditation to a group, when a neighbor suddenly started to mow the lawn while listening to loud rock music. I invited people to do listening meditation. At the end of the day, some people told me that the noises had been terribly disturbing and others that when they opened to the sounds with direct awareness, they felt very spacious. The sounds were the same for all the participants but it was their attitude with regard to them that made the difference. Some people, by grasping at the sounds negatively, tightened around them and experienced them as impinging on their space and consciousness. By holding onto the sounds as unpleasant they held them fixedly, thereby giving them more power of disturbance. Other people, by opening to the sounds, diffused their power of disturbance. The sounds blended in to a whole environment in which nothing was rejected.

We must be careful not to equate meditation with sitting in a silent room. I *welcome* any sounds when sitting in meditation as tools of awareness—they help me to come back to the present moment, sitting, standing, walking, hearing, being alive with a great potential. If I listen meditatively, sounds are not intrusive. They become part of the music of life. They remind me of my connection to the world.

On the other hand we have to be careful of using a noisy ambiance as a means to stop us from being aware of and listening to our thoughts, feelings, or sensations. The modern world seems to be full of sounds and music on purpose, to distract us or to soothe us, and silence then can become threatening. How can we find freedom and ease in listening to silence as well as to the sounds of life?

Words of Influence

Whenever someone speaks to you, notice how much you are influenced by her words. Certain discussion shows on TV can have the same effect. One moment you feel quite fine and the next moment you feel angry toward somebody who has not done anything to you but about whom another friend, perhaps, had been bending your ears strongly. If someone tells you negative things about someone else, unless you are strong, you will be influenced by their words. If someone criticizes you repeatedly, you would have to be exceptionally stable to not be influenced negatively by these words and feel bad about yourself. This is one of the gifts of meditation: to help you be fully present in a stable, steady manner. It enables you to be as grounded as a mountain but at the same time as vast as the ocean. These are the qualities we are trying to cultivate whenever we are listening to someone.

Once at a meeting, someone accused me of being bossy and told me repeatedly to stop organizing everyone. It was rather painful to hear but I took it on-board, striving not to feel bad about myself, but to look at the situations in which it was useful to be organizational and those in which it was better to let go of that tendency. When I investigated that habit of mine, I could see that I was practical and down-to-earth and this could come in quite handy. But when the pattern was rigid and magnified, it would become bothersome to other people and it could make me difficult and tense.

Another time a co-worker accused me in strong language of all kinds of things. As he was saying this it was clear to me that this had nothing to do with anything I might have done or said. So I listened without disturbance because I could not identify with it. At the same time I could see that he was in full flow and nothing I would say would make a difference so I just waited for him to finish. At the end of his attack, I calmly agreed to disagree and left. Later on he apologized profusely, which I accepted.

What is it that helps you to remain stable and open? In which conditions are you strong and confident, in which others not? To focus in meditation will help you to be calmer in general and so to feel stronger and more stable. To cultivate enquiry will enable you to encounter situations not one-dimensionally but multi-dimensionally so that you are not stuck where you find yourself but can respond creatively.

Smelling

We can be in the same situation of grasping and holding on with odors and smells. If our olfactory sense works properly then a cornucopia of smells opens to us. This can be a great gift if we are attentive to them. We can enjoy the heady perfume of flower blossoms, the spicy fragrance of a close friend, or the rich smell of baking bread. With meditation we can be more fully aware of smells in that by not grasping at them we can actually be more present to them.

I love to try new things and I also love perfume and fragrant smells but I am allergic to perfume and cannot wear any. So whenever I am in an airport, I am challenged by these two combined patterns of attraction and experimentation when I walk by the duty-free perfume counters. As I experience the contact of the perfumes through the olfactory sense, the temptation to try them out, just a little bit on the wrist for fun, is great. I can feel the strong movement toward it; it is like a physical pull. But this is my airport meditation practice, to resist the lure of the fragrances while being fully conscious of it. This is the test of encountering and smelling without physical ownership, without wanting to make it mine, without grasping.

We can also practice with unpleasant smells. I have a neighbor who regularly burns plastic rubbish on a little pile in her backyard. We have asked her not to do this but it seems this is the only thing she is allowed to do by law with that type of small plastic rubbish. So it has become my smelling meditation. When the smell of burning plastic wafts toward me sitting on the terrace, I just notice it, as it comes and goes. I do not exaggerate it or proliferate with it—though, like anyone would be, I am pleased when the small fire has been burnt through, and I can breathe fresh and clean air again.

Eating

When we eat, grasping often happens. We eat a slice of chocolate cake and it will be hard not to have another slice if there is the opportunity. How often do we feel heavy and stuffed and regret taking more than our stomach can handle? This is a difficult one because it meets our patterns of survival. We need to eat. Over time we can develop healthy patterns of eating: knowing what to eat and how much. But we can also develop destructive habits of eating when we eat too much or too little or the wrong things for our body.

It is very easy to eat too much, to eat more than your body needs. Grasping is the mechanism that will make it happen. You see young children do it—eat what they like repeatedly until they get ill. When you are eating too much of something that you like, you are grasping at the good taste that you experience but you are also grasping at the idea of the happiness that is associated with the taste. If you bring meditation to eating, you become aware of the color, the smell, the texture, and the taste of the food. You are conscious of each mouthful and you do not eat to fill yourself up but just to eat *fully*.

Grasping at Newness

Eating can teach us something about grasping at newness too—and how exhausting it can become. You might have a favorite dish, for instance, which you have not eaten in a long time. One day you taste it again and it is as though you were eating it for the first time. It is a wonderful experience—such a wonderful taste. It feels like new, like you have never experienced that dish in that way before. You make the dish again exactly in the same way or you go to the same restaurant, but the experience is not the same. You cannot recover that ineffable something that dish had that day. What you cannot recover is the newness of the experience. As soon as you have experienced something anew, it will never be new again.

As Thai master Ajahn Chah mentioned, if we ate a delicacy like bamboo shoots or asparagus everyday, it would not be a delicacy anymore; we would get used to it, we would look for something different, something new. It is likely that we keep trying to find exciting new things all the time and then move to the next one and the next one because one after the other they become old experiences. Whenever we try to repeat them, we do not get the same special experience of that first encounter, of that first moment. Can we move from a pattern of excitation to a response of appreciation? Each moment of life is a mystery; we are able to breathe, to see, to hear, to smell, and to taste. We are complex organisms alive in this moment. Can we recover the beauty of that, the sheer mystery of this life?

Once my five-year-old niece was staying with my mother in the flat below us. One evening she suddenly appeared when we were resting listening to classical music after working in the garden. She looked at us and said that she would dance. She then danced to the music of Schubert for the next thirty minutes while we watched her. She checked that we were attentively watching her and we enjoyed looking at her dancing, listening to the music while sitting quietly on the sofa. It was a very special moment between her and us, very loving, warm, and appreciative. Then she left to eat and go to bed. The next day she came up again and she wanted me to put some music on so she could dance. She tried to dance but it was not right, and I had to change the music several times and still it was not right. The following days she tried again. It was like she was trying to recover the exact beauty of that moment; but that moment was unrepeatable and could not be recreated in the same way.

We have to be careful that we are not trying to create a new experience with old ingredients. Each moment can be a new exciting moment if we open to it afresh. Each loved activity or food can be enjoyed if we do not grasp at it in a fixing way. If we try to open ourselves to the relatively same elements within the flux of time and conditions, we can enjoy what can happen, being open to it being the same or different. This is not a blind, superficial, or abstract acceptance but a creative acceptance, which is interested in interacting fully with the moment in its fluidity and its myriad conditions.

MEDITATION INSTRUCTIONS
Listening Meditation

Try to sit stable like a mountain and vast like the ocean.

Listen to the sounds as they occur.

Do not imagine, name, or analyze the sounds.

Just listen with wide-open awareness.

Let the sounds come to you and touch your eardrums.

Go inside the sounds and notice their fluid nature.

If there are no sounds, listen, and rest in this moment of silence.

Notice how sounds arise upon certain conditions and disappear upon others.

Do not grasp at any sounds.

Do not reject any sounds.

Just be aware of sounds as they arise and pass away.

Open yourself to the music of the world in this moment, in this place.

In your daily life notice the positive and negative habits you might have in your approach to listening.

What helps you to listen fully and spaciously?

If you are in a place that is very noisy, how can you help yourself? Must you find a quieter place or wear earplugs? Or can you be with these sounds in a different way?

See if you can learn to move freely between being in silence and with sounds.

4 Mental Habits

All experience is preceded by mind,
Led by mind,
Made by mind.

THE BUDDHA

 ## In the Grip of Thought

When we meditate, we can become aware of our patterns of thinking. We start to see how they affect us, and how they hold us in their grip. As human beings, it is wonderful to be able to think, reflect, imagine, plan, and discriminate. These are inherent functions of our mind. And we are lucky to have them. But often when a thought appears in our mind we identify and grasp at it, run with it until it seems to run us. We become easily obsessed with certain trains of thought. In some cases, thoughts can even paralyze us physically.

When my husband and I decided to settle in France after having lived abroad for thirty years, I did not realize the amount of paperwork that would be required to regularize our situation. One day I felt totally overwhelmed by this bureaucratic situation. I was finally presenting what I thought were the necessary forms to the officer in charge of national medical insurance after having unsuccessfully tried for a year to get medical coverage. After examining my files carefully she told me that it was incomplete and could not be processed. She added that she could see me again in two weeks time. I came out stunned and stood paralyzed on the pavement with feelings of hopelessness and discouragement.

The thoughts in my mind were: "This is hopeless. I cannot do this. It is beyond me. We will never get medical coverage." Fortunately wisdom reasserted itself and I started to examine these thoughts and feelings with meditative awareness. This created a space in which the grip of disempowerment began to relax and other possibilities opened up before me: "Wait a minute, I am not unintelligent. I can fill out a form. I just have to do it steadily, carefully, and patiently." This was a turning point in my form-filling odyssey. Since then I fill out forms with a lighter heart.

What struck me afterward was the powerful effect that grasping at the thought "this is hopeless" had on my whole body. I stood immobile on the street for a few minutes, people having to go around the obstacle I created. It was very painful and incapacitating to reduce myself to a single line of thinking: "This is hopeless, I am hopeless, everything is hopeless." If one holds on to this kind of thought tightly, there is no way out, one is stuck and goes deeper into feeling stuck because by grasping at these thoughts one stops life from flowing, moving, and creating. Meditation helped me by bringing me back to the fullness of being alive in that moment. I am more than my thoughts at any given moment. I have abilities and functions that can be activated: I can read, I can write, and I can try again.

Often several habits will fuse together to make things worse. It is true that I am not keen on bureaucracy or filling out forms, adding to the fact that I like things to happen quickly and efficiently, and thus these ingredients combined together make me react strongly to being thwarted by bureaucracy. The more I stick to what the self likes and wants, the more I react to any impediments in its way. I was reasonably healthy, I had enough money to buy any medicine I needed; medical coverage could wait another two weeks, even a month or two. Our idea is that things must happen now, otherwise it feels like the end of the world. The problem is not so much with the obstacle or impediment as with our grasping as to how it should be or happen, which then stops us from being adaptable and makes us react automatically instead of responding creatively.

Questioning

We can be defeated before we even start a project by just an idea: "I cannot do this. I cannot handle this." When we repeat this to ourselves, we are in the grip of a negative mental pattern. When the habit strengthens, it is like an illness, it actually stops us functioning and having choices.

I saw a TV show on a woman addicted to shopping. The test was for her to go into a shop and not to buy anything. Her idea was that she *had to* shop and when she tried not to, it was like a physical pull. I could see the power of desire in the wild look in her eyes, attracted to what she could not buy. Creating space by questioning in a meditative way can help us go back to the healthy functioning and activation of our senses and thinking.

We can cultivate a positive and creative questioning attitude of mind by learning to ask a simple question: *"What is this?"* When we do this in meditation we are not looking for an answer, we are not speculating, analyzing, or inquiring scientifically (a more detailed explanation of this questioning meditation occurs at the end of this chapter on pages 64–65). We are just opening ourselves to the moment in its array of possibilities.

We are actually throwing the question to the whole moment with an open awareness: "What is this?" We try to remain for a while with the pregnant sensation of questioning created by asking this question. As soon as it dissipates, we throw the question again: "What is this?" The question is like a diving board, which helps us to plunge into a pool of perplexity.

By taking the question as the point of focus you are cultivating concentration and as such a certain calmness and spaciousness. By questioning repeatedly in a lively manner like a child wondering about something they have noticed for the first time, you develop vividness and brightness in your whole being. If you meditate in this way, over time, your mind will become more flexible and you will start to see that actually you have more choices in action and behavior than previously you thought you had.

You can engage creatively with thoughts by knowing what you are thinking and realizing that you have come into contact with a new thought. Without meditation, when a thought emerges, it is so fast and intimate that you do not question it, you are not even aware of it arising. You just think it and act according to what it seems to dictate to you to say, do, or feel. When you meditate, sitting quietly, trying to focus on the question, you start to notice what takes you away from the focus; generally it is thoughts of one kind or another. The meditation is not intended to stop you from thinking but to help you discover what you think and how you think.

Inner Language

When you look at how you think, you can notice the language in which the thought is expressed inside your head. You are talking to yourself most of the time. There is a constant commentary going on in your head. What shape does it take? How

47

is it expressed? It is interesting to look at the overall feel/taste/color of it. Is it light or dark? Is it frothy or deep? Is it gloomy or joyful? Is it grey or bright? What is the texture of the stream of mind?

Are we using a language in our mind that is tentative, soft, and open, or are we using a mental language that is harsh, strict, and compulsive? We will feel differently if in our mind we are using repeatedly, *I must, they must, it has to be, it cannot happen, they should, he never, she always.* The more we use this kind of language internally, the more we will feel tension and rigidity—especially if things do not go according to plan. If instead we were to use more tentative language like *I could, he possibly, it might, they sometimes*, we then will start to encounter reality and circumstances with a more open and creative attitude. We'll begin to be open to things going one way, but also happening in a different manner as well.

Experience the difference you feel if you think, for instance, "I must go to see this concert" versus "I could go to this concert." With the first version you will fight and strain so that it must happen at all costs. With the second one you are open to it and will rejoice if it happens but if it does not, it will be fine. We can be so stressed by minor things that if we could bring less grasping to our thinking process, we would better evaluate what is essential and not so essential. When grasping becomes a predominant pattern, we end up grasping at everything the same without wise discrimination. Creatively engaging with our mental patterning would enable us to modulate more widely our response to different conditions.

Specific trigger words will set off certain patterns of thought. Everyone might have a different list. But there seems to be some fairly common ones like *fair/unfair, right/wrong, mine*. Notice what you think, say, and feel when the thought "This is unfair" rises up in your mind. Often you feel like stomping while repeating several times, "This is unfair." And a litany of "It should be this way" comes out. This is a rather frustrating and pointless exercise. Questioning meditation could help you examine your idea that things should be fair, balanced, and equilibrated. Indeed it would be nice if it were so. But life and the world are not necessarily like that.

Instead of stomping the ground helplessly with rising anger, it could be more fruitful and creative to look at the situation and ask: "What *could* be done here? Is there something I could do to bring more balance?" When we think: "I am right. This is right," how do we feel? What is set off in our being? Generally it leads to tightness. Do we grasp at the word *right* or do we use it for the sake of language? If we grasp at the word *right*, it will act as a trigger to our fixing and solidifying patterns. If we just use it because it is relevant to the situation, it will not have the same charge and disturbing effect. When you think "mine," does it lead to "It is mine and nobody can have it" or to "I am using this but you can borrow it or have a go"? By looking and inquiring into our inner language, we can start to play and experiment with it in a creative way.

Daydreaming

The next thing to look at is our mental habits. If we meditate, soon we start to see that there are definite patterns to our ways of thinking. We have a tendency to think repeatedly in the same way and this in turn has an effect on how we feel about ourselves, what we say and what we do.

In Korea I used to sit in meditation ten hours a day, three months at a time, so I had a lot of time to discover my patterns of thinking. After a while it finally dawned on me that instead of meditating I was spending a lot of my time daydreaming. I used to make up fairy-tale stories—about myself being a kung fu expert or about becoming enlightened. I tried to learn kung fu and lasted an afternoon—dreaming about it was much easier. I had to let go of that particular script. I think that this habit of daydreaming came from my childhood; I used to create long, complex stories in bed before falling asleep—possibly as a means to fall asleep, to occupy the time, or to distract myself from the fear of the dark. Whatever the reason, it became a habit that, when I became an adult, became linked to other parts of my life.

Imagination is a function of the mind, but daydreaming is a proliferation of the imagination with disadvantageous consequences. It makes you abstracted from what really is happening and it can lead you to feel frustrated because what you daydream of often does not happen. After all, for all my dreaming of becoming a champion in kung fu, I was not even keen on exercising and did not like being told what to do. There was no chance of it ever becoming *real*. When it is about kung fu it does not matter much, but if you daydream of a wonderful husband, job, a house, or even some imagined better life, it can create feelings of frustration and resentment.

Meditation can also make you discover the specific taste of thoughts. Daydreaming is very seductive; when the thoughts "If I were . . . , if I had . . ." come up, they pull you in; they taste yummy like something sweet and gooey, with promise of enchanted moments. If you are a prisoner in a jail like the men we met in South Africa, then daydreaming is vital, it helps them to survive. But as I was discussing this specific pattern of mind with a young prisoner keen on meditation, he told me that he would daydream in moderation and only used it as a safety valve when he felt very oppressed by his incarceration. If he did too much daydreaming then he became frustrated and aggressive. So it is not that we *cannot* daydream, but to see the effect this pattern has on us and to know when it is useful and when it is detrimental. When we ask the question "What is this?" it will bring us back to the moment. What is happening now? What is right here to enjoy and to appreciate?

Rehearsing and Plotting

Another habit that can be revealed when you meditate is *rehearsing and plotting*. Generally it starts with a memory popping up about something somebody said or did that was painful and you start obsessing about it—about how unfair it was or how painful it was. This actually brings pain from the past into the present—pain that was not actually there when you started the meditation. So you hurt and you obsess, and repeat the past event in your head. After you have done this for a while, you move to the future and you plot revenge, repeatedly trying to find the most cutting words or the most cutting things you could do to whoever hurt you. It passes the time quite successfully but it is not very fruitful or beneficial. It brings unnecessary pain and you plot for little purpose, as when you meet the person next it is very likely that they are not going to do or say what was in your mental script.

The difficulty with mental rehearsals of discussion is that they are in "mono-reality." You are the only actor in this mono-reality with a script based on an unchanging past that does not take into consideration that life moves on and that people and situation change. It would seem more useful to cultivate calm and flexibility of mind so that when you meet the person you have the tools required for that encounter—steadiness and creativity. You can prepare yourself when you are going to have what might be a difficult or fraught encounter, but the preparation is not about mental rehearsing but rather how to cultivate a grounded, spacious, intelligent self that can creatively engage and respond to whatever will come up.

Fabrications

Another painful pattern of mind is *fabricating.* This is when we create stories in our mind, which feel real to us even when they are not actually taking place. The texture of this habit is shakiness. There are tremors, uncertainties, anxieties, and fears in this pattern of fabrication. It often starts with the thought or words: "What if this happened? What if this is happening?" Then we create a story, which makes us feel terrible or sad.

For example, once someone on a retreat told us at the end that she had spent a whole afternoon thinking that her cat was dying because the friend assigned to the cat was not feeding it. Tears were in her eyes and her heart was breaking at not being there when her cat was dying. But of course it was totally made up; the cat was perfectly fine! Yet she spent more than four hours on this sad scenario—until she suddenly saw the senselessness of it and let it go.

This habit can affect a whole life. Consider a person who, for thirty years, was afraid that at some point someone dear to her would die and that would be the end of her world. She went about her life but in the background there was this pattern of fear: "If this person dies, my suffering will be unbearable." She lived her life under this sentence. Then finally it did happen and what was incredible to her is that although she was sad, she was also totally fine. She did not fall apart. Life went on. She was so surprised and so regretful that this had hampered her life for so long for no reason.

Often we are more afraid of the *idea* of something happening than the actuality of it. When we are actually confronted with it, we are able to deal adequately with the direct impact of the situation. Why is it that we are more afraid of something imagined than something lived? Something imagined can be greatly exaggerated by the power of grasping and fixing, and then we diminish our potential which cannot be manifested in abstraction. When we are in the situation itself, our potential can be accessed and liberated in the multidimensional encounter with the moment.

The opposite effect happens with "positive fabrication," in which the benefits of whatever you imagine with desire becomes exaggerated and glowing. But it is rare for reality to match that glow. This is the *if-only-I-had-that-I-would-be-happy myth.*

Recently I read an interview with a young woman who had always wanted to be a singer. She went on a TV show, nearly won the contest, made a bestselling single, and was asked how she found being a singer and her newfound fame. She replied that she found it stressful and did not think that she was going to do this for too long. Now she was thinking of becoming a psychologist instead!

Daydreaming, plotting, or rehearsing and fabricating are patterns of *mental proliferation*. An idea, a thought, a word comes into the mind where it can proliferate unmanageably in different ways.

Judging

There are other mental habits that are more like patterns of *behavior*, in that they color the mind in such a way that they directly influence what you do. One example of this is *judging*. If you have a mental pattern of judging, there is this running commentary in the mind about yourself, others, and the world. You put yourself outside of your being, like a judge on his bench, and pass continuous judgments on what is happening inside and outside of yourself. It can be quite tiring to pass constant judgment, night and day, with no time off.

Of course there are times when we need to be alert and able to react quickly to dangers, and at such times our discriminatory abilities are very helpful. Indeed, we are lucky to have that natural wisdom and throughout our life the capacity to refine it. In fact, meditation is a tool to deepen the creative power of this innate wisdom. But this ability to discriminate can be aggravated and exaggerated by self-consciousness, by regular criticisms in childhood and other detrimental conditions. Then it becomes a mental habit, which weighs heavily on our mind as it stops us from being closely aligned to experience by placing us above it.

Meditation can help us see that we do that, and help us not to judge it, as the judging of the judging—in an endless regression—is not going to be helpful. When we work with the judging mind, we need to be soft and gentle with these patterns but also steady and firm. We ask continually, "What is this?"—and by doing that we return to the full experience of the moment: the air on our cheeks, our feet on the ground. We experience that we can think in a generous and open way, trying to be present and conscious of our whole being, not living just through our discriminating faculty but with all our senses.

Comparing

Nearby to the habit of judging is the habit of *comparing*. We compare ourselves to others either positively—*I am better than they are*—or negatively—*They have a better life than I do*. When we compare positively, it can have different consequences. It can help us to rejoice and appreciate our happiness and good fortune, and make us more compassionate and open to others less fortunate than us. However it can also make us feel guilty about our good fortune and actually be a weight for us. This can happen to people who have inherited their fortune. It can also make us arrogant and dismissive of others who, we might feel, have not tried hard as we have.

Comparing is a natural thing to do; it is part of the evolution of competing for scarce resources. It can lead to competing for power or to competing to be the more generous. In some cultures, the greatest honor and respect goes to people who are the most ostentatiously generous.

When we compare negatively, we see what others have that we don't or that we want, we feel a deep sense of lack, of missing something, an unappeased sensation of hunger. It is a painful way to live—only looking and noticing what we don't have. It can make us bitter and profoundly unsatisfied. It gives us tunnel vision, which takes away any enjoyment or happiness that could be possible for us or is happening for us. Cultivating appreciation can help to dissolve the power of this pattern.

Appreciation, rejoicing, and gratitude are qualities that enrich our life. To appreciate the fact that we are alive and breathing, that we can think, that we can make contact with others, that we can feel the sun or the rain on our skin, is essential to our well-being. In order to rejoice at the happiness of others and share it with them, the Buddha suggested to practice the following phrases toward others: "May your happiness not leave you, may your good fortune not diminish, may your joy continue." When people practice with these phrases, over time it helps them to recognize and be grateful for their own happiness, good fortune, and joy; it also contributes to them rejoicing at the happiness of others.

Planning

Planning is a habit that can be extremely repetitive. We do not plan once or twice, we can spent hours planning, repeating the same idea hundreds of times, even trying to remember what we plan so we do not forget it. This is a pattern of control. As we do not want to be surprised by what life throws at us, we prepare ourselves in advance. This is a natural function of the mind that enables us to work with the future. But when it turns from being a useful function to becoming a pattern, it shapes our behavior and occupies our mind inordinately. To understand and work with this pattern of planning, we can begin to count how many times we plan anything. Then we can try to cut back to planning anything only *five* times. If we do this meditation exercise, we start to see that a lot of our planning is unnecessary and unproductive.

I do not need to plan ten more times six months ahead what I am going to put in my luggage for my summer holidays. I do not need to plan fifty times what I am going to wear for a special dinner one afternoon, a month ahead of the occasion. Actually you can put the seed of planning into incubation by just reflecting for a short period two or three times about what needs to be done. The appropriate plan will come of its own accord when it is necessary. We do not need to repeat ad infinitum plans in our mind. We need to trust in ourselves, in our capacity to deal adequately with the situation when the time comes closer.

Measuring and Counting

A subtler pattern of thinking is *measuring* and *counting*. How do I measure up? How happy, wise, compassionate, clever am I or have I been? It is like when you were children and your parent measured your height, where were you in connection with the decisive benchmark? Were you above? Then you could feel tall and proud. Or were you below? Then your head would droop as you had not measured up.

What is your mental benchmark for happiness, wisdom, and compassion? Often meditators feel bad because they are not mindful enough or wise enough or compassionate enough. Who decided where the benchmark is? Do we need one? The mental benchmark will be abstract and as such unrealistic. We cannot fit a description in a book. We cannot fit an image in our brain. We cannot fit the apparent happiness or compassion of someone else. We can only do the best we can at any given moment and try to learn from our mistakes.

Counting is another common pattern. We count the money we have in the bank. We count the number of days left before we have a holiday or a meditation retreat, or before the *end* of a holiday or a retreat.

I remember my first three-month meditation season with Korean nuns. The aim was for the two of us, Western nuns, to learn to be proper Korean Zen nuns. It was extremely difficult at different levels—mental, cultural, food-wise. I remember vividly the pain I would experience when I tore the page of the calendar each day, counting the days down and feeling that there were still so many left. I remember the worry of counting my dwindling money when I was traveling in India before I became a nun in Korea two months later. I was totally obsessed, on the bus in Nepal, amid the beautiful landscape, not seeing the landscape but only counting money in my head. I think that it was one of the reasons why I became a nun. Not that it would resolve my money problems, but I hoped that the meditation would help me deal with this obsession with counting and measuring. Again counting and measuring is a useful skill in construction work and when doing our accounts, but we need to be careful that it does not become a pattern that obliterates anything else in our experience and in our potential.

Meditation and Obsessive-Compulsive Disorder

Obsessive-Compulsive Disorder (OCD) is mental patterning in its most extreme and incapacitating form. A person suffering from OCD is obsessed with certain repetitive thoughts accompanied by feelings that something terrible will happen if these thoughts are not acted upon. This then leads the person to act repetitiously, compulsively. These actions actually do not relieve the discomfort of obsessive feelings or the thoughts, so the sufferer of OCD feel she has to *continue* them and thus becomes truly caught in a vicious circle.

On a retreat, I met a young man who had this disorder. In one private interview, he mentioned that although it was dark, he could not put the light on because he was afraid he would compulsively flip the switch for a long time. He felt that the meditation was helpful in diminishing the intensity of the thoughts and feelings, though they were still present. It also allowed him to see his obsessions and compulsions more clearly and enabled him not to identify with them so much.

Another young man I met on a retreat had suffered previously from a severe obsession-compulsion. He meditated assiduously and he also found it very helpful and supportive. His condition had been greatly relieved by the practice of the method developed by Dr. Jeffrey M. Schwartz, a research professor of psychiatry at UCLA and a long time meditator in the Mahasi Sayadaw tradition of Burmese Buddhism, which puts great emphasis on awareness and *mental noting*. This is a practice in which you consciously note what is happening in your experience without identifying with what you are noting. Inspired by his practice of mindfulness and the effects he saw it has, Dr. Schwartz developed a new treatment for OCD. Its foundation is a combination of cognitive-behavior therapy (CBT) and mindfulness. It consists in four steps:

Relabel
Reattribute
Refocus
Revalue

The patients doing his program are encouraged to "*Relabel* their obsessions and compulsions as false signals, symptoms of a disease." Then they need to "*Reattribute* those thoughts and urges to pathological brain circuitry." Following this they will "*Refocus*, turning their attention away from the pathological thoughts and urges onto a constructive behavior." And in the end they have to "*Revalue* the OCD obsessions and compulsions, realizing that they have no intrinsic value, and no inherent power."

One patient doing this practice realized that her symptoms came from hyperactivity in her brain and said: "It's not me, it's my OCD!"—this is the event that led Dr. Schwartz to call the first step of this process "Relabeling." When one relabels, one may still have unpleasant feelings and thoughts but they are less engulfing. Then one can relate to them differently and this, in turn, gives a powerful feeling of freedom.

Dr. Schwartz recognized that relabeling was not enough. It had to be followed by reattributing. Anna, one of his patients, said: "Once I learned to identify my OCD symptoms as OCD rather than as 'important' content-laden thoughts that had to be deciphered for their deep meaning, I was partially freed from OCD." With relabeling one sees more clearly what one is experiencing and reattributing strengthens that view. Reattributing is realizing that OCD is not willed but is related to biochemical imbalance in the brain. To know that it is OCD and that it comes from a brain misfiring is not enough. The power of the misfiring and misinterpreting is quite strong so one needs to refocus on some other activity to diverge and redirect the flow of energy, of will and intention. The activity must be habitual and pleasant so it is not too difficult to do. It must be active rather than passive; gardening or walking would be much more effective than watching television.

This step demands will-power and great commitment as the intrusive thoughts and feelings are quite powerful, especially at the beginning of practicing the program. Dr. Schwartz recommends the Fifteen-Minute Rule. Whenever someone has a compulsive urge he tells him or her to wait fifteen minutes before engaging in the compulsion, and do something creative and positive instead during these fifteen minutes.

Revaluing helps the patients to see the urges and feelings differently. They are not what they seem to be. The patients in that way develop wisdom, they recognize the thoughts and the feelings as not fixed and solid but dependent upon conditions. If they stand firm and observe the thoughts and feelings with mindfulness, refocus on some other activity with awareness, and revalue with wise attention, the obsessive thoughts and feelings will pass. Over time 70 percent of patients find that the four steps help them. Dr. Schwartz has found, through examining PET scans, that practicing the four steps actually diminished metabolic activity in the part of the brain that is hyperactive in obsessive-compulsive disorder.

Meditative Creative Thinking

At times it can be useful to do "meditative creative thinking" if you have something on your mind that keeps coming up: a choice to make, a decision to take, an important discussion to have. Every day you could think about that subject for half an hour. You sit and you concentrate fully for half an hour on that subject, without being distracted by anything else. But instead of doing what you usually do, which is to repeat what you have thought before about it, you think differently. You bring enquiry into your thinking process. You try to think of something about this subject that you have never thought before. You try to imagine how someone else would think about it. You are endeavoring to bring alertness and creativity to the subject in question. At the end of the thirty minutes, you let go of the subject completely for the whole day, knowing that tomorrow you can take it up again. In this manner you give time to what is on your mind but at the same time you do not let it invade your whole mental space. You could do this during one of your regular meditation periods, as long as you do not exaggerate or proliferate, or in addition to that period depending on the time you have. This is not exactly the same as meditating but sometimes you really need to bring a focused and questioning awareness to this kind of important topics.

Level of Mental Habits

It is important to notice that our mental habits have different levels of activities. They can be intense, habitual, or light. They become intense when something happens that is surprising, shocking, exhilarating, or hurtful. This will trigger the obsessive nature of the pattern. Then we feel invaded by the pattern and we cannot think about anything else; it is like an imprisoning loop. We cannot step out of it; we cannot create any distance or space within our mental faculties. We just obsess and the story goes round and round in our mind.

It is essential there to see that we are not always like this and that this situation was provoked by a definite incident. The power of the reaction often is so strong that the only thing we can do is to create minute spaces in the loop for a few seconds. We do this by asking the question "What is this?" and then grounding ourselves physically in the moment by being aware of our feet if we are walking or the sensation of our hands on each other if we are sitting. Or we can say to ourselves gently: "Let it go; let it be for a few seconds" and then try to imagine that we are resting our whole being on the physical experience of the breath—in-breath, out-breath, in-breath, out-breath.

When nothing has happened specially, but we're still following our habits, then the mental patterning is habitual—like judging for example. In this case, it is important to see the habit in action, to notice its effect and to loosen its power. You dissolve the power of the habit by not feeding it, which means that you do not proliferate or identify with the judging. You bring it back to its natural function by using one of the tools of awareness; that is, you focus on the breath, the sounds, or the question to come back to the whole experience of the moment. You can use any method of meditation that seems to help you create more space and openness and enable you to restore the un-patterned functionality of your mental abilities.

Light mental habits are natural. A live brain is active, constantly firing and thinking of something. We will have aimless trains of thoughts, weird association of ideas, shopping lists or light planning. These are interesting in so far as, due to their lightness, we can play with them more easily and also laugh at them as we recognize certain motifs and see how unnecessary they are. I used to have a "transforming old clothes" loop until I saw it clearly and was not taken by it anymore. Now I can see a "preparing luggage" loop. Since I recognized this loop, I only indulge in it near to the time of departure and not for very long. Having become aware of it, I find it pointless, as I know that I am quite able to do my luggage quickly and efficiently without endless cogitation beforehand.

We need to recognize light mental habits because under certain circumstances we move quickly from light to habitual to intense and we find ourselves in the grip of an obsession, which just started as a faint wisp of thought in the mind. We do not need to be afraid of our mind. We can go on a journey of discovery and experiment. Then we are able to play with our mental processes and develop our mental ability in wisdom and compassion.

MEDITATION INSTRUCTIONS
Questioning Meditation

"What is this?"

You can ask the question in tune with the breath: breathing in, I am aware I am breathing in; breathing out, I ask: "What is this?"

When you ask "What is this?" you are opening yourself to the whole moment.

You are not asking about anything specific. The questioning is open-ended. This meditation is about *questioning*—not about answering.

You are not looking for any answers when asking "What is this?"

No analysis, no speculation. You are asking because you do not know.

Try to develop a sensation of questioning.

Try to remain stable and alert.

You are focusing on the question within a wide-open awareness.

Experience the pregnant vibrating sensation that the question evokes.

Open to the moment fully through the question.

In your daily life, try to use the question as a way to re-center yourself so that it becomes a question that brings you back to the full awareness of the moment—body, mind, and heart.

Try to use the question when you feel stuck in a thought. Look at the thought and ask: "What is this thought?" You do not do this to resolve or analyze the thought but to question deeply what you are thinking in this moment. People find that when they question their thoughts in this manner often the thoughts lose intensity and sometimes even disappear.

When you do this meditation, sometimes an answer might appear: if it does, just let it float in your consciousness without grasping at it. If you get something similar to an intense sensation of questioning, just be with that in a stable way; if you feel unsettled by the sensation, stabilize yourself with focusing on the breath again.

5 Lost in Emotions

A disciple of the Buddha, mindful,
Clearly comprehending, with his mind collected,
Knows the feelings and their origin.

THE BUDDHA

Disturbing Emotions

Feelings are so intimate and immediate, and feel so real and solid that we often cannot imagine how we could transform them or engage meditatively with them. However if we shift perspective and start to experience feelings, like sounds, as unpredictable, coming upon conditions, fluid and changing, we might be able to encounter and respond to them in a different way. To know our feelings, to experience their texture, their effects on our body and thoughts enables us to explore the mechanism by which they become emotional patterns and then become exaggerated into disturbing emotions.

Each person has his or her own emotional patterns. People are described as kind, aggressive, or passive even when they are not exhibiting these emotions because over time they were observed as being repeatedly loving, angry, or indifferent. Some people in difficult circumstances have a tendency to sink and others to fight. It depends on outer conditions but also on inner feeling streams. If one is not aware of these streams, they will expand and make one act reactively and blindly, and lead to pain for oneself and others.

When we are in the grip of a strong emotion like anger, fear, loneliness, or grief, it is so encompassing that we feel over-whelmed and disturbed. It colors our whole being—body, heart, and mind. Sensations can reinforce feelings, which are reinforced in turn by thoughts. Feelings, sensations, and thoughts come together in a powerful mix to create disturbing emotions. If we look closely at feelings, we can see them emerge and metamorphose into these disturbing emotions. We can also start to recognize the feeling patterns that con-tribute to them becoming disturbing emotions.

Once I woke up feeling strange, a little grey and somewhat low in mood, which is relatively unusual for me. I looked around in my circumstances for why I would feel that way. I could not find anything. I saw this as an opportunity to explore this feeling. There were sensations in the body, which were somewhat unpleasant, but there was no hook in the mind to identify with them and exaggerate them. For the next two weeks I observed this feeling, which showed me that it was possible to observe feelings in the same way one would sounds. This low feeling dissipated when I met someone in great difficulty. I opened to that person with focused attention and compassion. The power of compassion was stronger than the energy of that feeling and it totally disappeared.

By not feeding nor identifying with this grey feeling, I did not create the conditions for it to become a disturbing emotion and then transform into an emotional pattern over time. To feel sadness when someone dies, anger when confronted by injustice, anxiety when in a difficult position, fear when there is danger, loneliness when one is on one's own for many days are natural responses to specific circumstances. As a human being, it is essential to have the capacity to feel—to cry and to laugh. It enriches our life and our relationships.

Sadness .

I used to see Master Kusan cry in two situations: when he officiated for the death ceremony of people he knew and when he talked to lay supporters about the "ten gratitudes" one needs to cultivate toward one's parents. It would not last long, just a few tears and then he would resume his normal composure. I was moved to see that a Zen master could be sad and cry in public, but also inspired by the fact that one could have feelings without being overwhelmed or disturbed by them.

Master Tahui, a twelfth-century Chinese master, replying to a disciple's letter, wrote this: "I take it that your fifth son is not recovering from his illness. It is precisely when afflicted that you should carefully investigate and inquire where the affliction arises from. If you cannot get to the bottom of its origination, then where does the one who is afflicted right now come from? If you want to think, then think; if you want to cry, then cry."

Master Tahui is acknowledging that his disciple is sad and in pain. He suggests four different ways of dealing with these feelings. The first is to inquire into the sadness itself, its form and shape, and to see if he can discern what is at the root of it, what is its source. If it is too painful to do that, then he can look at himself in this moment. Who is he? How did he come into being? By so doing he can see that he arises out of a flow of conditions and that everything that is conditioned is impermanent. If he cannot do that, he can think about his son and the joys his son had brought to his life. He can reflect that illness can happen to anyone at any time and he can also appreciate that he is able to be with his son at this difficult time. But he can also cry and express his sadness at the fact that his son is very ill and may be dying.

When I saw my father die, I felt great sadness but also in that intense emotional moment I experienced fully for the first time the reality of impermanence. Thereafter I started to relate to people in a different way, because I knew for myself how precious they were, that their life rested upon a single breath, the last breath I had seen on the lips of my father.

When someone dies, we are sad for a life ending but even more so for our loss, that this cherished person is no longer in our life. At that moment, if there is a habitual feeling stream of lack, of something missing in our life, the feeling of sadness, which is due to circumstances, will expand, spread, and connect to an emotional pattern of hopelessness or meaninglessness. It could be called the Poor Me syndrome, which expresses itself with such thoughts as: "I am alone in the world," "nobody loves me," "nobody is there for me," "I lose everything of value," etc.

This is a painful loop that seems to exist at least in some form in most human beings. It can be easily triggered by a simple feeling of sadness and can quickly take us down into the dark hole of hopelessness. It is quite painful and paralyzing and at the same time we seem to wallow in it—"Poor me, poor me, life is so terrible." I wonder if we wallow in it because although it is a painful state it absolves us of any responsibility. We become like a helpless child again and there seems to be an odd comforting feeling about this.

Can we see through that "Poor me" spiral and catch it before it starts and takes us down? It is difficult to be with unpleasant feelings: we do not like them, they are painful, and we want them to go away. But we need to know them because otherwise we will be caught and blinded by them and moved swiftly from the unpleasant feelings caused by certain conditions to being lost in the disturbing emotions that follow and are reinforced by the emotional habit.

Feeling Tones

One of the meditations recommended by the Buddha is to be aware of the *feeling tone* of one's experience, the tonality of one's feelings: is one experiencing a pleasant, unpleasant, or neutral feeling tone? It is quite difficult to do because sometimes it can be hard to pinpoint exactly what one is experiencing at the level of the feeling tone. Eating ice cream, for example: the sweetness impacting on the tongue could be pleasant but the cold impacting on a sore tooth could be unpleasant. Wind on the face as one is walking in the forest could be pleasant if one is hot and unpleasant if one is cold.

In order to become more aware of feeling tones and how they make us act and react we can try to notice how we respond to different feeling tones. After spending a wonderful weekend with friends, when they are leaving you will often say: "Let's do this again." At that moment, you want to recreate the same conditions in the future in order to experience the same pleasant feeling. When we experience pleasant feelings we want them to continue or to have them again. So we spend a lot of energy trying to recreate the same conditions in which the pleasant feeling happened, but there is no guarantee that the same feeling will be produced again.

The automatic pattern with an unpleasant feeling tone is that we recoil and do not want to have it. We do not like it, we would rather it passed us by and that somebody else would have it! And if we say to ourselves: "I cannot stand this," this will magnify the unpleasantness. As soon as we have pain and feel that we cannot stand it, the pain seems greater than ourselves, its border greater than our being, so much so that we feel we cannot contain it. But if we look at it directly, meditatively, it is broken in its various components, conditions, and circumstances and we can deal with it adequately.

When focusing on the feeling tones, bring the element of inquiry by noticing the sensations in the body and looking deeply into them. When you are at ease, how does that feel? When you are uncomfortable, how does that feel? You try to know and experience those feeling-sensations without grasping at them or rejecting them. You penetrate them in the moment without being diverted into a spiral of mental abstraction or letting them become disturbing emotions. You creatively engage with the feeling tone in the moment. If you do this repeatedly, it will enable you to pay attention and recognize more clearly the immediate feeling tone but also the habitual feeling stream of sadness, anger, or anxiety.

Before we describe or explain feelings to ourselves, how do they feel organically? What do we actually experience before we name them or are caught by them? Meditative awareness helps us to know and come into contact with that basic aspect of our experience of feeling. Sometimes we experience a strange feeling that is unnamable, it just feels *different*. If it is on the pleasant part of the spectrum of feeling tones, we may feel oddly buoyed, at peace and ease, and ready to take on the world. We do not question pleasant feelings because they feel good and natural. However it is essential to be fully aware of them, to know that we can experience feelings of ease and peaceful contentment. It proves to us that we do not *always* feel unwell and unhappy. If the unnamable feeling is on the unpleasant side of the spectrum, the challenge is to just be with it as it is without linking it so fast to one of our negative emotional loops.

Meditation on the feeling tones can help us bring more space and clarity around our feelings and make us see how changing, fluid, and ephemeral they can be.

Anger

Anger is hot, fast, and active. If we have a tendency to be angry, it means that we have a lot of energy. It can be useful to find a way to use that energy in a positive way so that it is not bottled up and then released in a destructive manner. There is a whole spectrum of angry feelings, from mild irritation to full-blown aggression, from mean words to murderous intention. Anger can be explosive or manipulative. It can come from being impatient, jumping to conclusions, or just blind reaction. My husband, Stephen, used to be a Buddhist chaplain in prison in England. One man he visited was in jail for murder. Stephen found him nice and friendly, and they had good exchanges together. He seemed to be an ordinary human being but prone to uncontrollable rages. If he found himself in certain situations, he would lose his mind and become very aggressive. He had no control over his anger and his behavior when he was caught in this pattern. Anger starts as a feeling, a natural response to being thwarted, contradicted, humiliated, or rejected. Can we find ways not to let it become a devastatingly disturbing emotion?

Anger shakes the whole body. It makes you red in the face. It accelerates your heart and shortens your breath. It makes your mind spin and lose control. You need to know it fully in order to be able to work with it, to diminish its destructive energy, to untangle the various mental and emotional patterns that give rise to its full-blown manifestation. With a meditative approach, instead of thinking that anger is your basic right (on the one hand) or the most terrible sin (on the other), you explore the inner and outer conditions that *give rise* to it and how it manifests itself. Then you can see what you are dealing with and start to work creatively with the different processes that constitute this emotional phenomenon.

Anger can result from an emotional pattern of impatience. We can learn to know impatience, to breathe into impatience, to inquire into impatience. How does impatience feel? It feels jittery and antsy. We need to move, something needs to happen. See how it feeds certain mental and emotional loops we have about the inefficiency, the uncooperativeness, or the insensitivity of others. Consciously or unconsciously we have a certain inner benchmark of efficiency, cooperation, and sensitivity that we apply to others and that feeds impatience and therefore anger. When we recognize this feeling and loop, if we stop and reflect that not everyone can be as efficient, cooperative, or sensitive as us, or that we are not like that always either, compassion and empathy can arise.

Frustration and feeling thwarted can also trigger anger. We need "instant satisfaction." When we feel thwarted, we become like a child, we cannot accept any obstacles in our way. We would like to have a temper tantrum so all that energy could be released. Those who have power can perhaps afford to have temper tantrums and shout at their underlings and thus will create a negative and disturbing atmosphere. Those who are powerless develop resentment, which eats into them and will come out in other ways to the detriment of others lower down the rung. It then creates a chain of disturbing emotions.

Fear is also a powerful cause of anger and aggression. Carl Upchurch, in his book *Convicted in the Womb*, shows through his life story how fear and survival led him to be a violent and angry young man. In order to protect himself from the violence of others, he became more violent than them so that they

73

would be afraid of him and leave him alone. This led him to prison several times and to do the same in jail—to be the "baddest" as self-protection. It is only through being sent to solitary confinement and reading repeatedly a book of Shakespeare's plays, used to balance a table with one shorter leg, that he was able to go beyond just being his fear and his anger. Only then could he free his potential and become a graduate from the University of Pittsburgh, a leading advocate for prisoner's rights and an acclaimed peacemaker. Fear and anger could then be transformed into concern for others and rightful action against oppressive conditions.

When we feel angry, we often feel energized—and that is one of its dangers. We can become addicted to this energy, so that we only feel alive when we are angry. This becomes a vicious circle. We react to situations in an angry way but we also provoke situations in which to be angry and feel aggressive.

However, it is possible to creatively engage with anger, and when we do, we can transform it and use its energy in a positive and beneficial way. When this happens, its power is harnessed and its tension dissipated. This can give us energy to work in the garden or clean the house, for instance, or to deal with a difficult situation in a firm way, or even become the defender of people who are unable to express themselves.

Feeling Low

If we have different habits, frustration will lead to feelings of *paralysis* and *stagnation*, which will turn into a mood of *hopelessness* instead of gathering energy into anger. Then we become listless and feel ineffective. We have the conviction that nothing is working and nothing will ever work. This feeling-stream is powerful in a negative way in that it makes us feel lethargic and without energy. It often starts out with just a faint feeling of being slightly low, not feeling like doing anything, then it morphs into not wanting to do anything and then into not being able to do anything. This is a very dispiriting mood to be in. It is not in general dangerous for others but very much for ourselves.

It is sometimes hard to come out of this listless state unless one has reached the bottom of it and then there is only one way, to go up again. However it is difficult to go back up from so deep down. It is for this reason that it is essential to be more aware of the low feeling when it *starts* and use creative means to alleviate it so it does not settle and spread. Because the feeling itself hinders any ability to do anything, it would be even more beneficial to catch it before it even starts to appear. As the Buddha suggests in two of the four great efforts: cultivate conditions so that negative states that have not been created yet do not arise and cultivate conditions so that positive states have the possibility to appear.

With anger, you have to create space; with low moods, you have to create energy. What is it that uplifts you? It can be as simple as walking or gardening. If I feel low or cooped up, I know that I need a good walk outside. Once I felt depressed in winter in England where it is pretty dark and wet at that time of the year. I felt that the solution was creativity so I went on a ten-week wood-carving course. It worked and made a big difference. I never did wood-carving again but it answered the need at that moment.

There are negative triggers but there are also positive triggers in your emotional patterning. There are the triggers that when activated will lift up your moods. It might not be the same ones all the time. You need to play and experiment. You have to be wise and creative at the same time. Some things might seem to lift your moods but not be beneficial in the long-run, like drinking alcohol or taking drugs. Other activities will help you to feel more buoyant without side effects—like walking, exercising, playing with children, singing in a choir, or gardening.

When you feel low, life can seem meaningless and if you have a habit of mental speculation you can then go into endless loops about the meaning of life and end up in the torment of existential angst. Great works of art have been produced by creative writers with this kind of angst, like Albert Camus' *The Stranger*. However, in terms of patterns and everyday life, it would be helpful to notice this tendency toward existential angst when in a low mood. It would be beneficial to see when it can be constructive and creative, and when it can become painful and destructive leading to nihilistic behavior where there is no hope and no care for self or others as nothing seems to matter.

This is why it is so essential to cultivate awareness—not a bare awareness that is *indifferent* to what is happening and is resigned, but a meditative and creative awareness that is deeply interested in one's own life and in the life of others. A kind and concerned awareness that accepts one's humanity and limitation but is also open to one's potential and its activation.

Boredom

When observing feeling tones, neutral feeling tones are quite difficult to pinpoint. However, if we look carefully we can notice that they can lead to two different feeling streams: one of ease and peace and one of boredom. Our modern society seems to be obsessed with entertainment, the assumption being that boredom is the enemy. We should not have the time or the opportunity to feel bored. Early on we can notice that children dislike feeling bored. This is one of their repeated complaints: "This is boring. I am bored!" I have a friend who is a stage actor who thinks it is essential for children to feel bored and to be able to deal with this neutral feeling. When his children complain about boredom, he tells them that it is very good that they are bored and that they need to practice feeling it.

Why do we dislike boredom? Is it that we find this feeling too close to death or that we find it difficult to be by ourselves with only ourselves for a companion? It could be so restful to experience that nothing is happening and that nothing has to happen. But boredom is not seen as a positive state of restfulness and non-activity. It is seen as the opposite of excitement and excitation. When we are in a low mood we feel bored, at a loose end, and everything seems tasteless. Can we cultivate being with neutral feeling tones in such a way that instead of feeling bored we feel alive? We could become aware of our breath moving in and out, of our heart beating steadily, of life coursing through our veins and we could take this as an opportunity to rest in the moment as it is, not good nor bad. This could help sharpen our perceptions of the different variations of feelings in our life, like a musical score. It would enable us to feel the whole spectrum of emotions from agony to ecstasy; and seen in that context, boredom can be very restful instead of a lowering down into a spiral of despondency.

Loneliness

When we are alone, we can feel at peace with no demands put upon us and the freedom to act as we choose or we can feel intensely lonely, unbearably so. If the condition of being alone becomes entangled with a low mood and a habit of feeling lonely, then there is the danger of feeling unloved or unloving. It can start with "nobody loves me" and finish with "I hate the world." At an essential level, we are deeply alone. Nobody can live our life for us and nobody can die for us. Nobody can experience our pains or our joys, though we can share them with others. How can we love ourselves so that we do not feel lonely when we are on our own? How can we connect to life and others so that we do not feel unbearable loneliness?

I am utterly alone but also intimately related to others, to the world and to life. My whole being depends on others and on factors outside of myself: the air that I breathe, the water I drink, the food I eat, the house I reside in, the clothes I wear, the medicine I take. My having been born depends on my parents and my ancestors. I am a tiny particle in an endless chain of evolution. My continued survival depends on society remaining relatively stable and peaceful. I am interconnected and interdependent with the whole world. My family, my husband, my friends, the baker, the postman, a Tibetan nun, and some African orphans depend on me.

It is important to cultivate relationships when we are not in a low mood so that it will lessen the effect of loneliness when a low mood comes. When you feel lonely, experience your breath, look deeply into it and remember that you are breathing with the people around you, and the animals and the trees. The whole universe is breathing with you. Remember that you do not need to feel afraid. You can connect and smile at the cashier in the supermarket who has had a long day of work. You can feel affection for a bird busily looking for food on the ground. You can remember the people who share your life and wish them well.

Anxiety

Anxiety is a strange feeling stream. It is an inner agitation that makes us feel uneasy and creates unpleasant vibrations in our whole being. If we are in a situation where we are on constant alert like soldiers on the frontline or if we live in a dangerous or constantly unpredictable situation, we feel on edge, constantly ready to jump. It is extremely hard in such situations not to develop a pattern of anxiety. Even when out of the situations, we still continue to feel anxious. It will take some time for the whole system to calm down and to feel safe.

But sometimes we feel anxious for no obvious reason; there seems to be this feeling of worry and concern about doing and saying the right thing, looking the right way, not being out of place, doing too little or too much. We need constant reassurances that we are okay and that everything is okay. The pattern could be of being too dependent on the outside world for our own sense of being. The eyes of others are not entirely dependable, and they make a perilous foundation for our existing. Finding a balance between self-sustaining and other-sustaining is conducive to feeling more at ease. We can benefit from others reflecting a positive image of ourselves but we also need to do this for ourselves. What is it that helps us feel confident and able? What is it that grounds us and makes us more whole and stable?

Meditation is not the only tool but it can certainly help enormously. In my own case, it has helped me greatly to accept myself, to grow and develop. It enabled me to stand on my own two feet, to fully inhabit my being and to trust in its possibility of expansion. Feeling stable and grounded is one of the keys to counteracting an anxious mood. When an anxious feeling emerges, see yourselves as standing solidly on the ground or sitting firmly on a chair and try to be with that feeling of anxiety without exaggeration nor proliferation. Become friend with the jitteryness; do not be afraid, you can be with this. Notice its wave-like motion; it is not exactly the same, it changes and fluctuates. Can you ride it skillfully and with agility, like a surfer riding a wave in the ocean?

Lack

Sometimes we experience a feeling pattern of lack, of emptiness, of a hole at the center of our being. It is oddly deadening and we do not know what to do with this hole, with this emptiness. It may be confusing for Buddhists who are told repeatedly that "emptiness" is a good thing, in fact the ultimate nature of all things or something like that—but the emptiness that is talked about in Buddhism is not an emptiness that deprives us of anything. It is a useful concept to denote that nothing exists independently and intrinsically, that we cannot reduce ourselves to anything, that we are a flow of conditions in constant motion. It is a constructive notion that helps us dissolve our selfishness, separateness, and isolation.

But this odd feeling of lack is different. It deadens and isolates us. It is important to try to discover the conditions that give rise to it. As it is an emotional habit, it repeats itself and we can begin to note when it occurs more acutely, when less, and when not at all. It is perhaps an ancient pattern of survival from our childhood that is not necessary anymore. How can that lack be filled? How can it become lighter and take on a different texture? Each of us has to look into our circumstances and try to find the keys or tools that could make a difference. With some people, it could be listening to music, filling themselves with sounds. With others, it could be painting, coloring that blankness, that void. Being with children or animals could help one to reconnect to a full life in a simple and joyful way. Otherwise can the darkness become like the night sky in which the stars can shine?

Meditation and Depression

When I lead retreats, I encounter people who have come to meditation because of depression. Meditation helps them to deal with this illness and its symptoms. However it is essential to see that each person is different. Some people can "treat" their depression just with meditation—but they are quite rare. Generally people with depression might take anti-depressants and often also see a therapist, and at the same time practice meditation. These three different methods are not opposed but, rather, are complementary. When someone is in the depth of depression, prostrate and incapable of doing anything, then one needs to take anti-depressants to emerge from the depth of the depressive state, reach a plateau in which one can start to be more active and *then* do meditation and go to a therapist. Depression is an incapacitating disease that has a tendency to recur and can become chronic. Sometimes the experience of a depressive state seems to create a groove in one's whole being.

Research has shown that some people who have experienced one episode of clinical depression will be likely to have further episodes. It is estimated that 50% of patients who've had one depressive episode will suffer again from depression at least once. If depression occurs more than twice, then unfortunately there is a 70–80% chance for depression to recur again and again. Some people seem to develop a long-term vulnerability to this disease. Some data from a five-year study point out that the sooner one relapses after recovery, the greater likelihood there is for depression to become a habitual condition.

Mark Williams, John Teasdale, and Zindel Segal, who specialized in studies of psychological models and treatment of depression, developed a maintenance program of cognitive therapy to prevent further relapse for people who had had several episodes of depression. (Cognitive therapy was one of the therapies found to be as effective as anti-depressant medication when dealing with depression.)

There seem to be many common points between Buddhist practice and cognitive therapy. They deal with and are concerned with the same material—namely human suffering and how to relieve it. They have in common a pragmatic approach that sees and finds a deep value in acceptance and compassion. Dr. Aaron T. Beck, one of the founders of cognitive therapy, believes that Buddhism and cognitive therapy share a commitment to self-responsibility and that both methods focus on immediate experience, trying to separate anguish from pain and use a kind of meditative awareness.

In the course of their research, Williams, Teasdale, and Segal decided to bring in the mindfulness approach of Dr. Jon Kabat-Zinn to complement the cognitive techniques. Over the course of a few years they developed what is now known as a Mindfulness-Based Cognitive Therapy (MBCT) program for depression, an eight-week course for groups of patients who have suffered several occurrences of depression. They found that their group treatment halved the relapse rate for people who had had three episodes of depression previously and was equivalent to other treatments if people only had had two episodes of depression.

In *Mindfulness-Based Cognitive Therapy for Depression: A New Approach to Preventing Relapse*, the authors state, "the MBCT program was specifically designed to reduce the extent to which patterns of depressive thinking reactivated by sad moods could feed the factors responsible for relapse/recurrence." They assumed that "such sadness-linked thinking resulted from repeated associations between the depressed state and characteristic negative thinking patterns within each depressive episode." They were afraid that "the strengthening of these associations with repeated episodes contributed to making relapse increasingly autonomous or automatic, so it took less and less to actually trigger the return of symptoms." Further, they thought "the preventive effects of MBCT arose, specifically, from disruption of those processes at times of potential relapse/recurrence." So they deduced that MBCT would be more effective with the "types of depression not so much brought about by unpleasant events but by prolonged rumination."

When I read the book on MBCT, I was struck by the fact that the course that had been developed was totally in accordance with the four great efforts as taught by the Buddha:

To cultivate conditions so that negative states that have not been created yet do not arise
To let go once the negative state is present
To cultivate conditions so that positive states have the possibility to appear
To sustain positive states once they are there

During the eight-week course the participants are taught various tools of awareness, mindfulness, enquiry, and concentration with an emphasis on awareness in the body as a means to take the focus and energy away from the negative mental ruminations that, combined with low moods, will trigger a depressive state. People are encouraged to explore, accept, and let go of their negative feelings and thoughts, and recognize and build on good feelings, their capacity for joy, and the ability they have to accomplish something of value and meaning.

MBCT is an important treatment that anyone suffering from depression should be aware of.

Conditions and Levels

As with thoughts, there are three different levels to the emotional patterning: intense, habitual, and light. When something sudden and unexpected happens, we are in shock and the emotion of anger or fear submerges us, taking over our whole body and mind. We can use this moment to know intimately in the body and mind the effects of emotion. Through regular meditation we develop the power of creative awareness; when it is strong enough it can make us penetrate deeply the emotions and their effects. When we see the pain that they cause us, over time we can dissipate the disturbing emotion and engage creatively with the feeling itself and the conditions that gave rise to it.

For example the other day I was on a plane in the United States. I touched the attendant lightly on the shoulder on behalf of someone else who needed something. She shouted at me not to poke her. I felt embarrassed and red in the face. I did not argue that I had not exactly poked her and instead I apologized. I felt intensely self-conscious but did not exaggerate it in my mind, did not let it proliferate. This event made me realize that airline attendants might not like to be touched even slightly because they come in contact with so many people. So although it was an unpleasant experience for me, I felt I learned something quite valuable.

At the level of habits, it is useful to start to recognize our habitual feelings and to see what we do to exaggerate and magnify them. We do not feel them all the time. What is it that makes them stronger and more repetitive? We need to see how we habituate ourselves. The more we are irritated the more irritable we will become. It is important to break this vicious circle.

The third level is that of being ordinarily human, feeling this or that throughout the day. It is interesting to notice how at the light level, feeling tones are changing all day long. You can actually see how you increase them; you can also experiment with trying to decrease them, or change them into something else, or play with the fact that they will naturally change by themselves. If something makes me impatient, if I believe the story line that started the feeling, then the feeling will increase. If I look at the conditions that created the feeling, often I see that my reaction is unreasonable because I want things to be different than they are at that moment when they cannot be, and then the feeling will decrease. This is something that I notice and ask myself often: "I am feeling this now, I wonder what I am going to feel in five minutes." Feelings are much more transitory than we think or feel that they are. Moreover when you try to find their core you realize that *they have no core* and are elusive and quite shadowy.

The way we feel does not depend just on inner conditions. Outer conditions also play a great role. It is important to notice what influences our emotional habits. Sometimes something as innocuous as a book or a film can have a great influence on how we feel. I do not read violent detective novels, especially at night, as it does not make for a good night's sleep. Literary or philosophical magazines are excellent to put one to sleep unless you are philosophically minded. I enjoy the buoyancy a good comedy gives me. When I come out of the cinema I feel like laughing and smiling; the world looks different. It feels oddly enchanted.

The meditative approach is not to avoid anything. It is useful to feel angry, to know how it feels, how unpleasant and painful it is. It is human to feel sad or joyous or anxious. Buddhist equanimity is not about having no feelings or only certain feelings. It is about creatively engaging with whatever feeling arises and weakening the power of disturbing emotions. I still get irritated and sometimes angry, even after meditating for thirty years, but it is much shorter in duration; the irritation lasts just a few minutes and then it is gone. I can smile, feel humble, and learn from having been lost in the habit again.

MEDITATION INSTRUCTIONS
Meditation on Feeling Tones

How do you feel at this moment?

Do you experience a pleasant feeling tone as you are sitting with ease?

Is the feeling tone somewhat unpleasant as you sit feeling a little agitated and restless?

As nothing is happening in this moment, do you feel bored? You could use this neutral feeling tone to rest in the calming rhythm of the breath.

Do you feel buoyant and happy? Try to experience and appreciate these feelings of happiness without grasping at those feelings.

Do you feel low and grey? Try to be with that feeling, knowing it fully without sinking into it or identifying with it. You are not reducible to any one feeling.

What do you feel in the solar plexus? Notice the texture of the feeling before giving it a name. Breathe softly into it.

If you feel a disturbing emotion, dissipate its energy by focusing on the breath or the sounds and relaxing the whole body.

Notice the story line in the mind that accompanies the disturbing emotion. See if you can let go of that story line.

Feel the whole body and mind as spacious and stable.

When you stand up, try to continue to be aware of feeling tones throughout the day in a kind and non-judgmental way. Remain interested but not self-obsessed. Notice if you are also intrigued by how others feel or seem to feel.

6 Signals of the Body

If one thing . . . is developed and cultivated,
The body is calmed, the mind is calmed,
Discursive thoughts are quieted,
And all wholesome states that partake of supreme knowledge
Reach fullness of development.
What is that one thing?
It is mindfulness directed to the body.

THE BUDDHA

Awareness of the Body

When we observe our body over time we can see that we experience bodily sensations that are relatively repetitive and recognizable. It seems that each one of us has certain physical habits conditioned by our biology, the impact of the world upon our body, and the physical activities in which we engage. For example I have regular difficulties with my stomach and my back. If I am cold and damp, my back will hurt. The origins of these patterns can be strictly physical but also connected to other mental and emotional patterns. If I become stressed my stomach is more likely to be painful.

Moreover the tendency of being lost in mental events and thus in abstraction leaves us with a disconnected relationship to our body. We depend on our body for our survival but we seem in some ways to prefer to ignore its existence. Often we use our body like a beast of burden, hoping that it will not give us any trouble and just perform its duty. Patterns of physical pains can be signals that the body gives us, telling us that something is amiss and needs to be considered.

In Korea I experienced my first attack of sciatica, acute pain caused by the compression of a nerve in the lower back. Coming back to Europe, I started to have sciatica regularly. It was painful but I could manage until I had it so badly that for three months I could barely sit on a chair. Reflecting on the physical conditions, I could see that, obviously, not everyone had sciatica and deduced from that fact that I must have some physical biological weakness, which predisposed me to experience it. Since I did not have the pain all the time, I started to look at the conditions that gave rise to that specific pain and to ask myself if I could do something about them. Was I stuck, doomed to have sciatica repeatedly?

I saw that sciatica happened if I was cold, when I was lifting something heavy, if I kneeled in a certain way, and when I worked in the garden too long. At that point I could have decided never to lift, kneel, garden, or be in a cold place ever again. But this would have created a pattern of avoidance, which would have brought on its own stress. I had to engage in these activities in a different way. But even before that, I needed to become more aware of my body in general, and not only when it was in pain.

To accomplish this Buddhist meditation on the body is a great tool. It enables us to inhabit our body and makes us conscious of it in a deeply felt way. The basic method is to cultivate awareness of sensations in the body.

Begin by doing a systematic scanning of the body from head to toe, starting with the head. Notice any sensation in each part of the body. Try not to grasp at or reject any sensation; just observe it impartially with careful interest.

How does it feel to have a scalp? How does the air feel on the cheeks? Slowly each part of the whole body is observed: the neck, the shoulders, the torso (front and back), the arms, the hands, the pelvic area (front and back), the thighs, the knees, the lower part of the legs, the ankles and the feet.

Don't make an effort to create or imagine sensations, just observe what it feels like to have a knee or a head. The sensations can be subtle and soft like the heat of the sun on the cheeks, or they can be intense like a sharp pain in the gut, or tight like a knot in the back.

Don't name or analyze the sensations, but rather try to just know them and experience them as they are. With concentration, focus on the physical elements of your being. Attend to your body, becoming fully aware and present to it. The body becomes the anchor into the moment. Be still and calm, open to the body as it is.

The body gives us the fundamental ability to experience sensations. Sensing is the primal way of being in contact and in relationship to the world around you and to your body. That relationship and experience of contact is connective. With inquiry, it is possible to experience the seamlessness of the sensation of contact. When we pay attention to the contact of our hands on each other for example, there is the sensation that one hand is in contact with the other seamlessly. We cannot say where one hand stops and the other starts. Being alert to that experience of connectivity through sensing enables us to see that we are not separate and isolated. We are connected to the whole world through our body. Although the body encases us, at the same time it connects us. With this meditation, we experience and understand this fundamental fact.

Penetrating Sensations

Meditative inquiry into the body helps you also to be more spacious when encountering intense sensations, especially of pain and discomfort. When you bring your attention to such strong or intense sensations, you look into them at an *elemental* level, without naming or identifying with the part of the body that is in pain, with the pain itself, nor with the fear or aversion accompanying the pain. If you penetrate sensations in this focused and questioning way, you will be able to experience their fluid and changing nature, which allows you not to tighten and grasp at them. In this way you will not reinforce or aggravate the pain.

Malcolm Huxter, a meditator and psychotherapist, describes this process: "When my attention could focus right into the center of the sensations with a quality of openness, I found . . . [that] the essential nature of the pain was space. Out of the space there were qualities of hardness, heat, movement and moments of burning, sharpness, pulling and twisting. All these elements would arise like miniature explosions out of the space only to change to something else and disappear again."

Once when I did a month silent retreat in Massachusetts, within three days I had difficulty with my stomach, which lasted the whole time. I was concerned about meditating so many days with this pain but decided to bear with it. When I sat in meditation, it was fascinating to see how changeable this sensation of pain was. Paying close attention to it, I would experience that its form and shapes changed all the time and also be surprised by its sudden absence. To see clearly that it was not solid, fixed, or permanent allowed me to feel freer with this pain and let me investigate the conditions that aggravated or alleviated it. By doing more lying down and walking meditation, the pain was less acute. By alternating the different postures, the pain did not solidify and become unbearable, and thus my possibilities for meditation were not extinguished. We have to be careful when using awareness meditation to attend to discomfort. Sometimes we can just watch it arise and pass away. At other times, we might have to go to a medical doctor to check that the pain does not indicate a serious illness. At other times, if the pain is too intense, we might not be able to bear it and then we might have to take painkillers, avoid or restrict certain activities.

The difficulty I have with my stomach is a physical habit. It is something I have had for a long time. It started with difficulty digesting certain food in childhood. Then in Korea I would often have pain in the stomach. My first reaction was to become lost in the *Why Me?* syndrome and then the *Poor Me* loop. Then I realized this was the suffering the Buddha mentioned as the first noble truth. The Buddha was not saying that everything in life is suffering but that there are many opportunities to suffer in life. I understood this truth experientially in Korea.

The Buddha taught that certain conditions gave rise to suffering. So where did my stomach pains arise from? Finally it dawned on me that they happened the most acutely during two yearly ceremonies while I helped in the kitchen. On these occasions, there was special festive food. I used to try things out and gobbled up what I liked. This was too much for my stomach. It could not handle the effect of the second noble truth—craving—in action. The physical symptoms were a signal to alert me to this painful habit.

I became more careful and attentive in order not to give in to the habit of curiosity and avidity so the pattern of gastric pain would not arise. It was more easily accomplished than I would have presumed. Intention and attention are effective tools for dissolving habits. This kind of intention is not to be assimilated with the list of good intentions we make at the beginning of a new year. To think it would be good to stop smoking or do more exercise will remain at the level of wishful thinking if it is not based on something concrete and deeply intended. Intention is powerful when combined with awareness and experiential wisdom. To be aware of our pain and conscious of the conditions that give rise to it make the situation concrete. If we intend to pay attention to these conditions, not with the aim of annihilating the conditions or the pain but of being present to what happens, then we can respond skillfully instead of reacting blindly.

I still experienced the desire for the tasty fried food on festive days in Korea; I could feel the saliva in my mouth but I did not act upon it because I knew intimately the pain that would ensue. If I ate the food, I would be consciously saying yes to being a slave to continuing the pattern. Intention gives us freedom of choice and is fueled by self-protection. Once we have intended and acted otherwise with the help of meditative creative awareness, it is easier to make that choice again and again. We are free from the habit unless we forget the intention and the possibility of choice and then the habit can reappear and act as a signal again.

Stress

I did not have acute stomach pains for many years after I left Korea. I thought I was relatively free from this physical habit until I experienced its psychological component. One day I was surprised to feel pain in my stomach again. Where did it come from? The food was fine in Europe and I did not overeat. But looking at my emotional and mental states, I saw that I was anxious because of planning our departure for our first long trip to South Africa. I was constantly mentally rehearsing packing the house and our luggage, and trying to remember what I should not forget. All this created an underlying stressful anxiety, which produced acidity in my stomach, and thus the pain. As soon as I became conscious of the mental worrying, I was able to let it go when I realized that this was what was causing the pain and also by seeing it was unnecessary. I needed to do some planning but not to worry about it. My task was to dissolve the exaggeration and the proliferation but not the activity itself. Thus I had to creatively engage with the exaggeration and the proliferation themselves, which meant mainly not to constantly remember to remember to pack this item or make this note.

When we start to understand our physical habits and their connection to our emotional and mental habits, we can learn to navigate among them in a less painful way. Stress is a combination of mental, emotional, and physical conditions meeting the outer environment. Its physical effects are signals to address what we are inflicting on the body. If we have pushed ourselves too hard, after a while our body reacts. There is only so much the body can endure.

In terms of stress, it can be useful to look at tiredness. What do you do when you are tired? Physical tiredness stresses your system. If you are the angry type, you become irritable; if you are the passive type, you start to feel hopeless. The feeling becomes the signal to the physical pattern. I used to find myself in irritable moods looking for targets for my irritation with unpleasant consequences for people around me, until I looked beyond the irritability and saw the tiredness. So now if I feel irritable, I look at the body first. If I see that I am tired, I try to find a way to rest, which has the effect of swiftly lifting the irritable mood.

Intense mental rehearsing can have a strong, stressful effect on the body and often people with this habit will be likely to have stomach ulcers. Intense mental fabrications can make us fearful and high strung, which also will have an effect on the heart. To succumb to a depressed mood will make one listless and keep one indoors so that one does not go outside and exercise. It was fascinating to watch a psychologist on television encourage a woman prone to obsessive behaviors and unfounded fears to go to the gym for an hour, and to see the difference that simple action made. The woman felt uplifted and her mood was radically transformed.

Mindfulness-Based Stress Reduction

One of the major components of Buddhist meditation is mindfulness. Mindfulness is the ability to pay attention and to be aware, and also the capacity to recollect one's intention. As the Buddha said in the quote placed at the beginning of the chapter: "If one thing…is developed and cultivated, the body is calmed, the mind is calmed, discursive thoughts are quieted, and all wholesome states that partake of supreme knowledge reach fullness of development. What is that one thing? It is mindfulness directed to the body."

Dr. Jon Kabat-Zinn, a scientist with a Ph.D. in molecular biology, as well as a writer and long-time meditator, developed a training program at his stress reduction clinic based on mindfulness meditation and yoga exercises. He experienced meditation and yoga as very useful for himself and conducted controlled research into this, which supported his own experience. He went on to create a very effective program, called Mindfulness-Based Stress Reduction (MBSR) which has been taught and is being used all over the world now. He has found that mindfulness can help people heal and have better health. He believes that with chronic illnesses and pains, medical drugs often are not enough. The patients need to be able to help themselves by becoming more conscious of their own body and also by developing inner resources to facilitate their own healing in collaboration with their own doctors.

He feels that "meditation catalyzes the work of healing." The people who come to the clinic have been sent because their doctor thought it could help relieve the stress that created or contributed to their disease. One participant, Peter, who had had one heart attack, came to the clinic to prevent another one. With the help of the awareness developed by the practice of meditation, he realized as he was washing his car late at night that "he did not have to be doing this." He saw clearly that he caused stress himself and could aggravate his physical condition by his habit of trying to do too much in one day. The mindfulness meditation helped him see and question this pattern so that he could cultivate different conditions and consider his time differently, not as a bank account dwindling, and his body as worth taking care of and paying attention to.

The clinic program lasts eight weeks and requires practice and commitment. The people who come to this clinic are in mental and physical pain and are looking for relief and a certain peace of mind. Kabat-Zinn and his assistants do a regular survey of the effectiveness of the program. They have found that meditation on the breath and awareness of the body are the most helpful techniques for most of their patients. The advantage of focusing on the breath is that it can be done anywhere, anytime, and it helps people calm down and be more present quite quickly.

At the stress reduction clinic emphasis is put on body awareness meditation and all the patients have to do it for at least the first four weeks of the program. It was found that this meditation was essential to give patients their first taste of ease and spaciousness.

In his own health routine, Kabat-Zinn has also found yoga beneficial. This is one of the reasons he incorporated in his program mindful hatha yoga, done very slowly with the emphasis once again on the breath and the sensation in the body as one did the movement. The mindful yoga exercises of the stress reduction clinic can also help the patients to have a breakthrough about their relationship and habits in connection with their bodies. The aim of these exercises is to stretch and to exercise the body in such a way as to strengthen it. Mindful yoga also allows the patients to become more aware of their limits and at the same time their possibilities. Often patients are surprised that they can do it at all and realize that they can be more flexible and strong than they had previously thought.

Some people have the habit of ignoring their body and over-exerting, other people have the opposite habit of being fearful and extra cautious in connection to their body, making it actually less supple and strong. We need to find a middle way between stretching ourselves and protecting ourselves. This is why a deep intimate awareness of our body is so essential.

Dealing with Chronic Pain

What to do when we have chronic illness and pain? How can meditation help? Wouldn't awareness and mindfulness make us *more* acutely aware of our pain and difficulties, and thus make it *more painful?*

When I teach meditation retreats, some people come with serious chronic conditions. Although the retreats are in silence, they enjoy sharing the space with forty or sixty people in a quiet, supportive, and safe environment. They participate in the schedule of the retreat within their own possibilities.

Some have to rest in their room, others have to meditate lying down. But all do the meditation because it helps them deal more compassionately and wisely with their suffering mentally, physically, and emotionally.

Chronic pain has a tendency to accentuate and sharpen your mental and emotional patterns. It is very difficult not to feel hopeless, cut off, isolated, ignored, unsupported, misunderstood, despairing when in constant, debilitating pain. In such circumstances your negative habits can become exaggerated. Then you have a double suffering, the actual suffering due to the illness and the mental and emotional suffering that surrounds your attitude to the illness.

In *Finding a Joyful Life in the Heart of Pain*, Darlene Cohen, a Zen priest and teacher who has suffered from rheumatoid arthritis for twenty-three years, explains how meditation, body awareness, and movement have helped her deal effectively and creatively with this painful and crippling disease. She feels that when we are in chronic pain instead of fleeing the pain we need to know it deeply and acknowledge the suffering it is causing us and at the same time balance this by developing our potential for happiness and discovery.

In her experience, "sensation is information about one's body." It is for this reason that awareness meditation can be such help. We learn to know our body intimately and become information wise about it instead of abstracting ourselves from our body. When in chronic pain she points out that we can have a tendency to grasp at the past that was not painful and thus negatively grasp at the present which is painful, not dealing with the pain effectively and actually reinforcing it.

When I am really tired or in pain, if I do not fight these conditions and accept them, stop doing, just lie down, read and rest, I experience ease and peace and generally will recover more easily—stress free after two or three days. After intense activities or a bout of illness, we need to listen to our body and allow ourselves recovery times and not fall into the fallacy of the pattern of doing: that we only exist if we perform at a high level and agitate ourselves all the time.

When Darlene Cohen started to explore the totality of her experience instead of reducing herself to her pain, she discovered a whole world of sensations changing and fluctuating. We can be lost in our pain and while magnifying it reduce ourselves to it, or we can experience the pain as one element among many that we can be aware of in any moment. If we practice with pain in this way, it will take us away from mental abstraction and keep us aware of our practical and organic existence. Then if with courage and gentle determination we redirect our attention to the whole of the moment, we can become interested and even charmed by the diverse elements in the moment like the sound of the rain, the moving shadows of the light on the wall near a window. Once I was in a hospital bed immobile for five days, I spent most of my time looking through the window at the sky and the clouds, and their shifts and changes. It was so vivid and peaceful at the same time.

MEDITATION INSTRUCTIONS
Awareness of the Body

Find a comfortable position lying down on your back on a blanket or pad on the floor or on a bed.

Close your eyes and relax, with the body long and the arms resting on the sides of your body.

Now pay attention to the sensations in the head: in the scalp, on the face, inside the head.

Be aware of the whole head without grasping or rejecting any sensations.

Then move your attention to the neck. Feel the skin of the neck, inside the neck.

Next focus on the shoulders. Notice the contact of the clothes on the shoulders, then the contact of the back of the shoulders on the floor or the bed.

Next move to both arms and hands, feeling their weight.

Next be aware of your back lying there. If there are any strong sensations, go into them and experience their fluidity.

Next move to your torso. Notice the contact of the clothes on your chest and the seamlessness of that experience.

Next become aware of your buttocks and any sensation in that part of the body.

Next move to the pelvic area. Do not name the sensations. Can you be with sensations as they are?

Next be mindful of your thighs, back and front. Consciously relax any tensions in that part of your body.

Next focus on the knees. If there is discomfort, do not grasp at it; just penetrate it without identification.

Next focus on the lower part of your legs and your ankles. Notice how sensations appear and disappear.

Next move the attention to your feet. Go inside your feet. Feel the soles of your feet.

Finally be aware of the whole body, its weight, its energy, its pulsation.

Before standing up wiggle the toes gently, rotate the shoulders and arms, rotate the legs and feet with awareness.

When you get up, try to do it consciously and mindfully. Stand a few seconds fully aware of the whole of your body standing there.

As you move to accomplish your tasks of the day, try to continue with the mindfulness of the body. From time to time, pay attention to your posture.

Try to be aware of how you handle and use the body.

Use the contact with the body as a way to take you out of abstraction and back into the organic world.

For example, notice the contact of your feet with the ground or the coolness of the wind on your cheeks.

7 Recovering from Addiction

The thought manifests as the word
The word manifests as the deed
The deed manifests into habit
And habit hardens into character.
So watch the thought and its way with care
And let it spring from love
Born out of concern for all beings.

ANONYMOUS

Addictive Habits

As described in the quote above (attributed varyingly to several different sources), the more we think a certain way, the more we will talk in a certain way and act in a certain manner. Over times these habits will grow in strength. When patterns turn into addictive habits, they can become deeply destructive.

Marc Valleur and Jean-Claude Matysiak, French doctors and specialists in addiction, talk of the peanuts effect. When you drink with friends generally you have some salted peanuts. You eat some, then some more, then some more. After a while you are full and you do not need to eat them anymore, but you still continue. Then you find yourself unable to stop. What they point out is that it becomes a habit that ends up being invasive even when the initial pleasure has disappeared.

The challenging questions are: What is it we need? What is it we want? When does simple need become craving? What is the bare minimum required? What is it we can live without? We need to eat, to drink, clothes to protect us against the cold, houses to keep us safe and warm, medicines to heal us. We also need to love, relax, and relate.

Desires, impulses, and urges can easily be clothed in the garments of need. We might feel we need to have more sex, buy more clothes, or have another bottle of wine. A need can destructively turn into a craving that is detrimental to self and others. There are so many different levels of needs and dependencies, some healthy and others not. What are these urges fulfilling, displacing, or replacing? With the help of awareness and mindfulness can we stop for a moment and enquire into the experience of addictive habits, explore the feelings, thoughts, and sensations that trigger and contribute to these habits? Can we engage with them in a more creative and sustainable way?

Patterns of Addiction

When we are addicted, we are locked in a pattern of desire and craving. The addictive substance or the addictive conduct touches all aspects of our life because it dominates our whole being—mental, psychological, emotional, physical, and spiritual. It starts to dictate our behavior and even our purpose in life. When this happens, we are not a free agent in our own life.

In England there is an association, the Prison Phoenix Trust, which is dedicated to teaching meditation and yoga to prisoners. This organization sends out a quarterly newsletter with one section dedicated to prisoners' letters. Often these prisoners are drug addicts and it is inspiring to see the liberating effect meditation and yoga can have for these men and women. One prisoner pointed out that doing meditation helped his recovery from addiction by allowing him to feel free and to no longer need to be in control of the world around him.

Part of the meditative path is to "watch the thought and its way with care and let it spring from love born out of concern for all beings." It is an injunction but it is also the effect of meditation. Meditation is something to be cultivated and at the same time in the cultivation there is the effect: in this case the opening of the self and the heart. It is striking to see this in these prisoners' testimonies. One man of thirty-eight who had been taking drugs since age fourteen wrote that when caught in his drug addiction he was uncaring and harmful to others. But recovering from his addiction and doing meditation and yoga helped him to see others beyond himself and to be concerned for them.

The prisoners found that meditation helped them to accept themselves and encounter their inner mental or emotional turmoil in a spacious and lighter manner. After leaving jail they continue to benefit from meditation. The patterns of mental obsessions and physical compulsions that led to addiction are hard to dissolve. But over time, it seems that meditation can contribute to creating a space within those patterns. Then people can start to experience something different, another dimension of their existence. They can discover that their capacities are greater than they ever imagined. But they need to trust and have faith in the potential for growth that is in each of them.

Meditation allows us to be more present—not in an abstract manner but in such a way that we experience the actual reality of being alive, breathing, standing, feeling, sensing in a more direct manner. Life then has a different feel. It seems to flow and has its own depth and riches.

Meditation and Recovering from Addiction

Meditation can help in recovering from addiction, but because addiction is extremely difficult to deal with and is in fact a life-threatening illness, the power of meditation alone is generally not enough to help one overcome it. It is for this reason that it needs to be considered a useful help in terms of recovery but not the only tool.

This is what writer China Galland found out when she was struggling with an addiction to alcohol. She started to meditate to help with her drinking. With Zen meditation she managed to control her drinking. But she found out later that doing meditation turned into another coping activity—like running or wilderness trips—which continued to mislead her into thinking that she was fine. She kept telling herself to just sit. But this felt like just suffocating her life. Because she could not admit to herself that she was an alcoholic, she could not admit it to other people either and did not tell anyone in her Zen group.

It is only when her fourteen-year-old daughter stood up to her and confronted her after she had drunk herself to oblivion one evening that she finally accepted that she had a problem with alcohol. She realized that she was unable to stop drinking by herself and that she could not manage this only with prayer or meditation. This was not active enough. She needed a program, steps to follow, and a supportive group. Joining an Alcoholics Anonymous group was a key element in her recovery. She tells how important it was for her to talk with others about her disease and also just to be with people who were sober. In the end she found that prayer and meditation (the eleventh step) were an essential link between Buddhism and the community of recovery. She thinks "of the sangha (community) of sobriety . . . as the self-arising of the Buddhadharma (Buddha's teaching), a wisdom called forth for our time."

In the Buddhist tradition we take refuge in the three jewels of the Buddha, Dharma, and Sangha. The Buddha represents at the same time the teacher and the awakening potential within each of us. The Dharma is the teaching of the Buddha as well as the way things are. The Sangha is the community of beings who support each other and who aspire to awakening for the sake for all. All these three elements are essential on the Buddhist path. We need to take refuge in all three of them in order for a beneficial environment to be developed and for our practice to reach its fruit: awakening and the manifestation of our wisdom and compassion to its fullest degree.

Many people have been greatly helped by joining twelve-step groups such as Alcoholics Anonymous or Narcotics Anonymous. Noah Levine, now a meditation instructor, wrote *Dharma Punx* and showed clearly in his memoir how he needed meditation but also the twelve-step program to help him overcome and leave behind an addiction to alcohol and drugs that made him aggressive and a thief. Although his father is a meditation teacher, due to the divorce of his parents and other painful and associated conditions, Levine took to drugs and alcohol and a life of violence on the streets. It is only when he reached bottom at seventeen after a failed attempt at suicide in Juvenile Hall that he started to turn his life around. In despair, he finally listened to his father suggesting that he try to meditate watching his breath. At the same time a young man recommended to him to read a book about recovery from drug and alcohol addiction. The meditation helped him to have moments of respite from his misery and feel peaceful, and the book showed him that other people suffered like him and that there was another way to live. Once out of Juvenile Hall, he made a new life for himself by continuing to meditate, which enabled him to become more mindful and calm. He also went to an Alcoholics Anonymous group regularly.

To have an adult sponsor for two years helped him enormously as well as actively taking responsibility and admitting his faults. These are powerful steps: to accept one's misdeeds, to see one is responsible for one's actions, to actively cultivate strength by facing up to one's hurtful acts. Meditation can be an agent for change when someone is recovering from addiction but it needs to be situated within a larger environment of support.

The Middle Way

One Buddhist model, which could support us in recovering from addiction, is *the ten perfections*. The ten perfections are ten qualities that could help us to build our strength so that we could continue to recover and sustain our move to the "other shore" of clarity, understanding, peace, love, and creative action. The ten perfections are:

Giving
Ethical behavior
Patience
Endeavor
Meditation
Wisdom
Appropriate Action

Vow
Strength
Understanding

To cultivate *giving* is to cultivate an attitude of generosity toward self and others. When we are addicted we view ourselves and other harshly and generally do not give ourselves and others the benefit of the doubt. As David Gregson emphasized in his book *The Tao of Sobriety*, it is essential to see ourselves as innocent. We did not wake up one day and decide to become an addict. It has happened to us. We need to be generous and giving to that part of ourselves that made us become an addict. We have to accept and recognize it in a giving and humble way. We also have to see that being addicted stops us from being generous to others. Being generous to others in practical terms and finding the time and space to give something to others helps us to move from self-centered addiction to a more sane exchange and relationship with others.

To *behave ethically* is to commit ourselves to a compassionate and caring attitude. It comes from the realization that our thoughts, words, and actions have consequences. If we harm, steal, or lie, it causes suffering to others but also to ourselves as we feel in conflict with the law and with a compassionate attitude. Generally it induces guilt, fear, and discomfort. Awareness helps us to recognize that drinking, taking intoxicants, gambling, or having sex in an addictive manner is destructive to our well-being and the well-being of others. To behave ethically is to be committed to be aware of thoughts, words, and actions and to consciously decide and act in a compassionate and caring manner to ourselves and to others.

Patience is the capacity to endure and to wait, to know that things are organic and will take time. We did not become addicted in one day and addiction will not stop overnight. Mental obsessions and physical compulsions are very strong forces. They will come up again and again. Recovery is a slow process of change and growth; we need to have the patience to take it one day at a time, even sometimes ten minutes or ten seconds at a time. Patience can also help us to see that we do not need to act upon every thought or feeling we have. With awareness we know thoughts and feelings, and with patience we wait for them to pass. First they will be strong but if we stand firm with a kind and patient mind, they will ebb and disappear more swiftly than we expected.

In *Scar Tissue*, rock singer Anthony Kiedis speaks of his life as an addict, how three times he went into rehab and twice he relapsed. The final time, back at home, one night he had some obsessive thoughts about taking drugs again. The feeling of wanting made him take his rucksack and go out of his house. Then he stopped by the porch and realized that he did not want to do drugs again. He knew in his bones where it would lead and he did not want to waste his life this way anymore. So he went back inside and the feelings passed. He learnt that he could be with this obsession until it went away. He found that by not acting upon his compulsion each year it has diminished in strength.

Endeavor is the determination to do something. It is the capacity that we all have to have an intention and to act upon it. It is more powerful than we think but for it to work it needs to be organic and not abstract. Endeavor is to see that we are matter and have energy and that we can act for the good. We can gather our energy, apply ourselves, and do something. If we reflect on the human condition, we realize that human beings have great capacities but in order for these capacities to be fully manifested we have to apply them in action, not to think about them but to do them. At the beginning it is hard because it seems to go against the stream. But the more we apply ourselves in a steady and not frantic manner, the more energy will come and it will become easier and less daunting.

Meditation is what I have described in the previous chapters. It is the conscious act of being aware and mindful. We stop and focus on the breath as a means to quiet the whole organism. We also listen in a calm and focused way as a means to develop the ability to be with sounds without reacting and letting them pass. It enables us to see and to be with the rising and passing away of phenomena. We can also cultivate equanimity meditation by reciting silently in our mind three phrases:

> *May I accept things as they are,*
> *May I know that actions have results,*
> *May I be at peace and balanced.*

This meditation will help us to live with the fact that things happen. We make them happen or they happen to us and we have to accept the situation we find ourselves in. If we find ourselves in a happy situation, we know it and we are grateful that in this moment in time things are going well for us. If on the contrary the situation is difficult, if we have troubles with addiction for example, we accept and recognize that it is so. This is the truth of the situation. This acceptance does not lead to resignation or despair but enables us to engage creatively with the situation at hand. By knowing that actions have results and that causes have effects, we see that specific conditions and actions will lead to certain results. Then it is for us to act upon this knowledge and to cultivate skillful actions, which will lead to more positive and creative results instead of destructive ones. We also wish peace and balance for ourselves, to recognize when we feel them, to see what kind of environment—inside and outside—helps us to experience them.

Wisdom is developed when you experience and know for yourself the changeability of events, the unreliability of things, and the conditionality of existence. If you are aware and mindful that thoughts, feelings, sensations, and events change then you are more ready to flow with these feelings and let the thoughts pass through instead of being blocked by them and finding them unbearable. If you neither rely on nor expect situations to be exactly as you wish them to be, but are prepared to see how they unfold, and if you are more open to the unpredictability of circumstances, you will be more flexible and respond creatively to them. If you see clearly that you and the world around you are constituted by a myriad of elements you will not so readily identify with and reduce yourself to one of these elements.

If you feel anxious or unhappy, you know that you can wait for this to pass—you do not need to fix the anxiety or the unhappiness immediately by taking drugs or alcohol. When some situation does not go the way you want it to go, you do not feel powerless or aggressive and turn to intoxicants, but you look for what you can learn from this or how you could understand it in a different way.

Appropriate action is the activation and manifestation of our creative potential. It is difficult to resist the impulse of certain feelings and thoughts if we cannot replace them with a more wholesome activity. To just remain in resistance is extremely tiring and undermining. We need to function, to use and activate our mental, emotional, and physical energy purposefully and positively not only for ourselves but also for others. Addiction is often isolating. So appropriate action requires not only that we do something creative to occupy ourselves but also that we relate to others.

It is essential to open our heart and to build supportive, caring, and respectful relationships—be it with our family, friends, acquaintances, children, ill people, old people, or people in need. There are many people in the world that we can encounter and meet. We need to be wise and to see which category of people we would have the easiest time relating to in a positive way.

To make a vow is to set an aspiration. It is to ground our life in certain values. It is to trust in our own potential or appeal to an outside power in which we believe. It is to have faith in something greater than what seems our limited self. However, aspiration is not expectation, to vow and to aspire is to give energy and openness to our life. Expectation on the contrary will set a definite aim and thus limit and constrict our possibilities. A vow states our intention and creates a current, which we can flow toward and feed. We can renew and extend our vow. It is helpful if the vow is not too extraordinary but at the same time helps us to stretch ourselves.

Strength is essential to fulfill our vow. Everyone has strength that they can use. We need to flex our mental, emotional, and physical muscles. It is in the exercising that strength can be developed. We try to push ourselves in a skillful way. When we are strong, we also have to remember to be stable and open. When we are recovering from addiction, we rediscover the strength and thus the freedom to act in a different way.

Understanding is knowing and experiencing that we can be at peace and that we can live a life of wisdom and compassion. It is a potential and also a reality. Everyone has moments of clarity and of altruism. We can experience peace, wisdom, and compassion. At the same time we know that these capacities disappear when we are caught up in destructive patterns of addiction. The more we experience peace, wisdom, and compassion, the more we will be able to recover from addiction. So when we are at peace, we rest in it, see how it feels, how it leaves, and how it comes back.

MEDITATION INSTRUCTIONS
The Five Methods of Transformation

These five methods are intended to help one creatively engage with the thoughts, feelings, or sensations one might experience at times when one is recovering from addiction or before the patterns of addiction might have totally set in.

When an intense negative thought, feeling, or sensation arises, try to replace it by something positive.

If you sense in your body the need to smoke, can you instead do some breathing exercises?

If you feel the desire to gamble on the internet, can you instead go outside and play with the children?

If you think about shopping compulsively, can you go instead to ask your elderly neighbor if she needs some help?

If an intense negative thought, feeling, or sensation re-emerges, please ponder its negative consequences.

If you feel like having a drink, can you remember the destruction that followed the last time you did that?

If you want to take drugs, can you see clearly the pain it will create afterward in you and around you?

When an intense negative thought, feeling, or sensation continues, distract yourself creatively from it.

Go for a run in nature.

Call someone who is sober.

Occupy your hands, doing embroidery or knitting.

When an intense thought, feeling, or sensation of addiction takes hold of you, look deeply into its felt experience and question it.

If you feel like smoking, how does this manifest itself? Could you feel something else?

If you think of shopping, what is the story that you are telling yourself? Can you have other thoughts?

If you have a physical compulsion, how is it? Where do you sense it? Can you use your body in a different way?

When an intense negative thought, feeling, or sensation re-appears, can you wait until it passes? Can you take refuge in something greater than yourself—like the Buddha, Dharma, and Sangha—to help you pass through this difficult moment?

8 Love

Tell me, What was Love Like?
Was it round or square,
Short or long or of a shape
One would be proud to wear?
I do not know. I only know
So far its fold extends
That none who knows its shape can say
Where love begins or ends.

Anonymous (from Korea, in the 16th century)

Love is a wonderful feeling. When we love we feel uplifted and joyous. I love snow. When it falls (rarely in the South of France), I feel buoyed and elated. I cannot keep still; I have to go out. I am happy to see the cat. It warms my heart to see him alive. When my husband is away, I feel that there is an empty space and that something is missing. Love warms us and lightens us.

Yet often we have a hard time feeling love for ourselves. Imagine if you could love yourself fully how warm and uplifted you could feel, since the object of your love would be with you all the time. But we don't feel this way. We have a strange habit of not loving ourselves. Why do we not merit our own love when we are the closest person to ourselves and depend on ourselves for our own existence?

Here two habits seem to unite with a conflicting effect: we have a tendency to be self-centered and at the same time we do not love ourselves. This means that we focus our attention on a being we do not seem to love and we feel stuck with this unloved person. There could be many theoretical explanations or external conditions for the causes of this situation. What interests me is not so much knowing the causes, but exploring the situation we find ourselves in. Any one theory cannot serve as explanation for the situation of every person. Often it is also too late to be able to do something about the causes: we cannot easily change our society, religion, or family. Moreover we cannot change something that has happened in the past. It is done and gone. The one thing that we can do is change the way we *look at* the past, not as a prison but as conditions that came together and happened, and transform the destructive habits we might be experiencing and feeding in this present moment.

We seem to not love ourselves in two main ways: through perfectionism and through negative judgment. If we have a pattern of thinking idealistically about ourselves, unless we are blindingly self-absorbed, we can never reach the mark, we can never fulfill that ideal and perfection—being the perfect mother, the perfect human being, the perfect worker, the perfect artist. We think that we need to be perfect to be appreciated and loved, and to appreciate and love ourselves. We can aspire to be a good mother, a good human being, or a good artist but if we have a fixed image of who we should be or even more of what we should have achieved by now, we will generally fall short. It is hard to compare ourselves to abstractions, be it an abstract idea of what should be or in comparison to someone else's achievements. We never know how the people feel within themselves; we only see their external apparent success.

At least the perfectionist will be looking up or urging himself up and then might have to come down a little from these lofty heights. The person who starts from a negative thinking and feeling habit is down already and will incline further down. "I am not good enough. I will never amount to anything. I am hopeless. Nobody loves me. I hate myself." These are very painful habits of thinking and feeling. The perfectionist has more energy than the negativist but in the end they find themselves in the same place—frustrated, discontent, and unlovable. We need to love, accept, and appreciate this human being in an ordinary way. We do not have to exalt it or to depreciate it. We just need to appreciate what is there and do what we can do with the material at hand.

My parents were kind, loving, and supportive to each other and to us, and I feel fortunate to have been born to them. However, in my early childhood, I did not feel so comfortable in my own skin. First I wanted to be a boy. Then I had to wear glasses, which led other children to call me by numerous negative names. Then my sister used to call me "potato," as she was much thinner than I was. This could be what made me shy and awkward (unless I was already born that way). If I were to give it a name, I would say that in my youth I had an inferiority complex. But it was not so clear to me; it was just this inchoate inner feeling of discomfort, of awkwardness and tension, especially around others. I felt at times that either I was the greatest or the worst. There was no middle ground. It seems that we oscillate between these two patterns of self-aggrandizing and self-annihilation.

It is only when I started to meditate and cultivate concentration, enquiry, and awareness that the tension inside started to dissipate and that I began to be able to accept, appreciate, and love myself for what I was and also what I could be. It was liberating to see that I was not fixed and solid, that my thoughts and feelings were not fixed and solid and that I could creatively interact with myself. I was not stuck in any position. Meditation helped to release the grasping on self and the false notion of the self as definitely this or that. In the space that was created by releasing this grasping, creative and healthy love for self could bloom and grow.

It is much easier to live with yourself if you love yourself; you have more peace, feel more contented and light, and also you can assume more easily the fact that your life is lived alone with others. By accepting and creatively engaging with the dimension of aloneness that comes with the human condition you stop feeling lonely and acting out of the pain of loneliness, which can bring difficult and painful habits in your relationships with others.

If we do not love ourselves, we create two difficulties in terms of relationships: either we cannot understand why anyone else would love us if we don't love ourselves or we need to be loved by others in order to feel alive and acceptable. One reaction leads to rejection or suspicion of others who are then forced to pass a series of tests to really prove that they love us. The other reaction means that we become needy and possessive for fear of losing that love which seems to be essential for the upholding and sustaining of our identity.

Falling in Love

When we fall in love with someone, we feel like we are floating; it is often said that we feel on cloud nine. We become totally obsessed with this person and our feelings for him or her. It takes us out of a multi-dimensional reality as we are caught in a reality of two people obsessed with each other. This is shared and reciprocated self-centeredness, which can be quite agreeable but possibly not functional. When I fell in love with my husband, for three days I was not functional and my inner feelings were very tumultuous and full of elation. But this falling in love state cannot be maintained; it is the newness and suddenness of the discovery that creates the excitement.

Falling in love is an experience, and like all experiences it has a beginning, middle, and end; it is not a durable state. If the attraction can be transformed into a sustainable feeling of shared love and if the appreciation between the two people develops, then love can grow between them. But if they grasp at "falling in love" and want this feeling to remain with its intensity and exclusivity, they will be disappointed. They will think that the disappearance of the intensity is due to the other person who was not as lovable or as loving as expected and then fall out of love and look for the next person to fall in love with. In this way one can become addicted to "falling in love" and be caught in a pattern where one will be unable to sustain loving someone over a certain period of time.

Romantic Love

Romantic love is an abstract love filled with dreams and idealization, consolidated by films, songs, plays, and certain cultural biases. It is rarely found in reality, as love in reality is multi-dimensional. Theories abound for why we fall in love with any given person. It is indeed mysterious. But loving someone, appreciating them for who they are and not what we want them to be, is not easy because of our self-centeredness and our mono-vision or perception. Each of us has developed many habits due to inner tendencies and conditions but also for survival purposes, to be able to endure this life when it was painful, difficult, and incomprehensible. When two people fall in love and decide to spend time together, two sets of habits meet and some sets might fit better than others.

In the Western world we are educated to strive for excellence through interpersonal rivalry and competition based on an adversarial approach. So often this is the pattern and ground on which love will be built. To this is added ideas about justice and fairness, and love becomes a competitive field where we measure everything. This is not an open and supportive relationship. We fight for what is "due" in terms of love. How often do we think or say: "If he or she loved me enough they would do this or that for me." We are easily disappointed in the other as he or she does not match our abstract romantic ideal. Life is not like a film on a screen, flat and illusory. It is complex and surprising.

Love is something to work on and cultivate. Many of our habits and patterns will work against the growth and development of love. We must be very careful because love between two people is precious and fragile. The intensity of falling in love misleads us into thinking that our love is strong, but if it is based on us experiencing a certain type of feeling it becomes very fragile. Because when we do not feel these feelings all the time, what do we do?

We can be so caught up in the habitual ideas, dreams, and ideals that we hold, that if something goes wrong or is difficult we can easily convince ourselves that the person we loved so much a few moments ago is so terrible that we cannot love them anymore. If we think this often enough, the feelings of love will not be nurtured and will disappear.

On the other side of the spectrum, we can fall in love with the wrong person: someone who is manipulative, hurtful, and abusive. If we are caught in the romance and the feelings of the romance, we might find it hard to accept that we made an error and love the wrong person. This will make us stay in the relationship and endure abuse for misguided feelings and reasons.

The appeal of abstract romance can work both ways, positively and negatively. In both instances it exaggerates the attraction or the repulsion of the person involved and stops us from dealing with the reality at hand—that the person is not so bad, which means that things can be worked out, or not so good, which means that we have to escape for the sake of safety, sanity, and health.

The Art of Loving

To love and to be loved is an art and a practice. It requires us to appreciate, care for, and accept each other. We do not love an abstraction; we love a multi-dimensional human being with his or her history, habits, tendencies, inner and outer conditions. We learn each other, grow together, and at the same time we can never know the other completely. Each person will keep a private garden, where certain inner thoughts and feelings can only be known to himself or herself.

Nowadays disclosure and communication are considered essential. Of course it is important to be able to talk and listen to each other, but too much disclosure can be misperceived and misinterpreted. We need to be wise and kind in what we say to each other—this is the wise speech of the Buddha. What do I say and how do I say it? What is the intention behind my words? Is it to clarify and explain, to hurt, to tell our truth no matter what? What is our truth? It is so changing and often self-serving. What does it mean to communicate when we love one another? If we keep everything in, we will become resentful; if we say everything that passes through our mind, it can be very hurtful. What is the middle way?

The middle way in a relationship starts by accepting and appreciating the other as he or she is. One of the greatest gifts we can give someone is to say yes to him or her. In loving him or her, we are also affirming his or her existence, that this person's presence in our life enriches our own existence. When we accept someone without condition then true love can blossom.

If you cannot accept someone unconditionally then you might need to creatively engage with the situation and consider the kind of love that would be possible to have toward your partner. If your partner is abusive, manipulative, and hurtful for example, and if he or she does not seem to want or be able to change, you might need to love him or her from afar. I watched a program on television recently on battered women and I was saddened by the length of time these women stayed with their abusers before they left. If someone hurts you or demeans you, this is not a proof or demonstration of his or her love or your own fault. There are no excuses for aggression in a couple. It might be painful to live on your own but never as painful as living under the constant threat of abuse and aggression. We do not need someone else to exist. Each person can exist in her own right by her own means and with her own potential to develop.

The Middle Way

The middle way in love is to accept each other—each other's qualities, each other's weaknesses. From this deep unconditional acceptance, we can work on understanding and transforming painful relationship habits in a creative manner. If we say to someone: "stop being like this or like that or I will stop loving you," we do not offer that person much choice. If we tell someone that certain habits that he or she manifests bring us pain, then we can discuss why and how and together we can see if there is a way we can be otherwise. What is the smallest thing that we could do together to make a difference?

I come from a large, close, affectionate French family while my husband's family is small, British, and more detached. I found it painful at the beginning of our marriage that my husband was somewhat distant and aloof while we shared a single room in a Buddhist community. First I had to ascertain why it did not feel right, what was the problem. Then I had to find a way in which he could experience what it was I was trying to point out.

I decided to play with it. Sometime I would be very affectionate to my husband and sometimes I would restrain myself and be more like him. After a while, he started to enjoy receiving affection and started to become affectionate himself. If we have never experienced something, we have to learn and experience by ourselves that it is a good thing. Words and discussions do not have the same effect.

When a couple encounters difficulties, they need to discuss and explore the source of the difficulties. I prefer to eat on time. My stomach digests better if the food is hot, and I find it uncomfortable to stay long at the table. My husband likes to eat very slowly, in his own time and does not mind his food cold. As we eat three times a day together we had to learn to adjust to each other's differences and find a middle way so eating times would not become a battleground. First we had to see that we had these habits, which meant that we did not do this on purpose to annoy each other. Also it was not a question of "if you loved me enough you would change to suit my habits." Habits are not right or wrong, when they are of the relatively neutral type and not causing excessive harm to someone. We develop them to suit our mental, physical, and emotional conditions in interaction with the habits of our family or society (though my husband is more French than I in his eating habits!).

When two sets of habits come together, as in any relationship, what happens: Conflicts and battles with a winner and a loser or adjustments and adaptation with love winning and growing? This is why cultivating the middle way for a couple is so important. We cannot totally change for someone else but we can adjust, understand, and play with differences in a wise and loving way.

A few years ago I realized that my husband and I had different survival patterns in stressful situations. For example, when we traveled, if difficulties arose, he would go slower and I would go faster. Until I realized these were different coping habits I had assumed he did it on purpose and was being obstructive while I was trying to rush us along. Now that I know, I am much more relaxed; I still press on but less frantically and he still slows down but not at such a snail pace and there is less tension and no blame. A love that is wise and accepting can help us to become more mindful and aware of each other in a non-judgmental way. We are not competing nor are we psychoanalyzing each other. When there are difficulties, we are focusing on the moment and inquiring deeply just like in meditation: What are we doing now? How are our coping mechanisms manifesting themselves?

Making Love or Having Sex

This is a difficult topic for Buddhists and meditators. When the Buddha taught two thousand five hundred years ago, most of the time he talked to celibate monks and nuns. So again and again he emphasized a life of celibacy as being conducive to awakening and the dissolution of desire, and he rarely if ever talked about sexual relationship in a positive manner. However in the *Sigalovada Sutra*, known as the layperson's code of discipline, the Buddha presented five ways in which a husband and a wife should mutually take care of each other, which include faithfulness, and five ways a child and parents should mutually support each other. So the Buddha did not say that everybody should be celibate, only those who choose the monastic life.

If as Buddhists or meditators, we reject sexuality in a blind way, our sexual desires will actually become detached from love and lead us into difficulties. This strikes me whenever I hear or read about the latest sexual scandal involving spiritual teachers. If we do not appreciate the power of sexual desire and the way it gets distorted by negative habits and if we do not combine it with love and commitment, it will often lead to pain and anguish for ourselves but even more so for others.

Being a monastic is conducive to being celibate as one is helped by the discipline and one's commitment to the monastic life. However it is not easy and at times one will be tempted to succumb to sexual desire either because one needs affectionate contact or one cannot resist one's sexual desires. A friend of mine told me how when she was a young nun, a Thai Buddhist monk tried to convince her to have sex with him by telling her she would boost her merits and would get a better rebirth! She declined the offer.

When one is a celibate monastic, one has to keep the rule of celibacy; if one cannot then one has to return to lay life. One of the great Patriarchs of Zen, Huineng, said: "Those who wish to train themselves spiritually may do so at home. It is quite unnecessary for them to stay in monasteries." One can be a practicing layperson, in a loving and committed relationship, and it is natural to make love in such a context. It is part of our energetic potential. We are biologically made for this. Making love does not lead us astray from the spiritual path if we do it with care and awareness.

However, many painful habits are linked with our ideas of love and sex. It is for this reason that it is important to bring awareness to our sexual life and to see if there are any destructive patterns of power, desire, and frustration in that area that leads to pain for ourselves and others. It is difficult to look impartially and objectively at feelings of sexual desire, they feel so strong and compelling and seem to call out to us to satisfy them. We do not have to act upon them necessarily all the time. Sexual feelings can come and ebb away like any other feelings and sensations.

You need to see how you grasp at those feelings, identify them, and then exaggerate and proliferate with them. You can try to be conscious of them and notice what happens if you do not do anything with them. Also you might have to look at how you generate them and increase them in a way, which might not be always skillful, by watching certain films or reading certain magazines. Sexual feelings add to and complement a deep relationship of love. They can also become destructive emotions and sensations that make us hurt others and disregard their own feelings.

Detached Love?

In spiritual circles there is sometimes the idea that to be truly spiritual you cannot love or only in a detached way. This means that you find many relationships where partners are so "spiritual" that not only are they unattached but also they are uninvolved and somewhat uncaring as they claim their non-attachment and spiritual space. These people still seem to need contact and sex, but only on their own terms. Sometimes they even need several partners at the same time.

I met one such person once. I was totally mystified; he presented very well in spiritual terms, said the right things at the right time and in the right way, which led one to believe that he was truly on the meditative path. Then I learned that he had had serial relationships and sex with several people in a very short period of time, in the same organization in which he was working, without telling any of them of their rivals in his supposed affection and sex life. Of course this created a lot of pain and anguish for everyone concerned when the situation was revealed.

When you love someone it is natural to develop a certain dependency on each other. A relationship is two sets of negative habits meeting but also two sets of positive habits encountering each other. Each person will teach something to the other due to his or her different interests and creativity. A new world will open and your own world will be enriched by the other's world. If there is true love, people will deeply influence each other for the good. Thanks to my husband I can think more logically, for instance, and thanks to me he is a better cook.

It is not "detached love" but "non-grasping love" that everyone, spiritual or not, should try to cultivate. Problems in love arise when we grasp at the person or the feeling the person creates in us. If we grasp at the person, this will make us want to be with them all the time. If we stick to them like a pot of glue, it will be unhealthy for both. One partner will feel crowded and imprisoned and the other who does the grasping will be unable to develop other friendly relationships with a diversity of people. So both partners will be stuck and unable to grow within the relationship and also outside of the relationship. As with any grasping we become restricted by what we grasp at. Love between two people is not a merger, it is a meeting and walking together on the same path.

Relating

Loving all kinds of people in different ways is essential as it enables us to come out of our self-centeredness and stretches us. It opens our whole being to a world of relationship, communication, exchange, affection, and warmth. Love melts inside us the fixed barriers we erect, and the feeling of solitude that can come with the human condition. By sharing the world with others we have the opportunity to love and bring warmth to our life and to their lives.

This became obvious to me when my grandmother declined so much in her old age that smiling to her did not produce the usual response of warmth and joy. She could not relate to us at that human level anymore. However two things were left that gave her joy: flowers and animals. She was always happy to bring us flowers from the garden when they were in bloom. Also when my niece brought her small fluffy rabbit, my grandmother would stay next to it all the time. It made her happy to be able to relate in a loving way to this animal. It seemed to be the last link she was able to open with another being, which helped her to come out of the isolation that her age and illness had forced upon her.

The opportunity to relate to and connect with another being is a gift that it is essential to nurture, be it with friends, family, children, or animals. What does it mean to be a wise and caring friend, an affectionate family member, a loving parent, and an animal lover? To develop friendships and relationships we need to see and care for the other for his or her or its own sake and not just for our sake. In order to be able to do that it is essential to develop creative, wise love, a love that is unafraid and also that is stable.

The Buddha, in the *Sigalovada Sutra,* described a warm-hearted friend as one who is a helpmate when one is in difficulty, who is the same in happiness and in sorrow, who gives good counsel and who sympathizes. Friendships for the Buddha were sustained by courteous speech, helpfulness, impartiality, and sincerity. The Buddha saw the development of friendship as an essential element of the cultivation of the path. We need the help and love of others and they also need our help and love. With meditative awareness we can explore the inner and outer conditions that help us to be good friends and to develop loving relationships. Certain habits will make this more difficult; for instance, if we are easily afraid it will be more difficult to trust another person and to relate to him or her in an easy manner.

It is for this reason that the Buddha developed loving-kindness meditation as an antidote to fear. If we develop loving-kindness and see the world in a more benign way, it will be easier for us to relate to the world more readily. When we cultivate loving-kindness, we wish for our own well being and the well being of others in a systematic and focused way. We strive to recognize the importance of each being's life and the need for happiness and joy for that being. In this kind of meditation we look beyond our habitual responses to self and others, which have become fixed and limited over time and we reach out to the part of us that is alive, breathing, and can be happy in this moment.

Another counter-productive habit in friendships is arrogance and self-importance. If you think that the friendships and appreciation of others is naturally due to you without any ideas of reciprocation and shared relationships then this will become a very biased relationship with no equilibrium. Moreover, it will be easier to be friends with people who share your views, ideas, perceptions, culture and who do not contradict you. But it is also revealing and enriching to become friends with people who are different from you in many ways. I find it rewarding when I become friends with someone from another culture who has different ideas and perceptions; it expands my universe and shows me the multidimensional potential of human being. It is so easy to be caught up and limited by our own preferred boundaries.

Family Bonds

Families are the basis and ground of any human life. Generally we spend twenty formative years with our family. Over time family patterns develop and are also replicated from past generations. This is the challenge facing any parents raising children: "Do I recreate how my parents raised me and how they lived or do I do something else?" My own parents married very young and were conscious of the difficult habits present in their familial upbringing. From the start, they decided that they would raise their children differently with more stability and affection but also openness and understanding. Early on I noticed that all our friends came easily to our house but we rarely went to theirs as the conditions there were stricter and we felt less welcome.

The social conditions of each new generation in the twentieth and twenty-first centuries have changed rapidly; often it seems hard to apply ancient mores and habits to new generations. At the same time the message of the Buddha coming across two thousand five hundred years still speaks to us and to our conditions when he speaks of the mutual responsibilities of parents and children to support each other and have compassion.

We do not, of course, choose the family we are born in; sometimes we are lucky and find ourselves in a stable and loving environment and sometimes we are unlucky and find ourselves in an unstable and cold environment. But even in a good environment we can develop destructive habits and in a difficult environment we can develop constructive patterns. Many factors come into play, inner and outer, when a child grows up.

What is essential is for the parents to accept that parenting is a mysterious task where they will generally try their best and sometimes fail. What is striking is that the living example of the parents will be more influential than their words or recommendations. My parents were against religion (which did not stop me from becoming a religious person) but in their actions and ways of being they were open, flexible, and loving, which affected deeply my humanistic outlook on life. Parents will influence their children positively and negatively but also the child is his or her own person with his or her own emotional, mental, and physical tendencies and qualities.

Meditative awareness can help us become more conscious of our assumptions and expectations of ourselves and of other members of our family. For a family to be harmonious there needs to be love but also cooperation and understanding. It is helpful for each adult member of a family to try to meet the other in the present and to look beyond the habitual vision that has been built over time. We aspire to reach out to the person in the moment as a human being with his or her fears, suffering, and joys. Once I could relate to my mother in this way, thanks to the creative awareness developed in meditation, our relationship became much easier as it enabled me to bypass the awkward habits that had been set. When with family members, this is my task—to meet them in the moment as they are now, beyond any fixed, habitual label.

Adult sons and daughters often feel that their parents do not really listen to them or understand them or want to understand them. It is important to see that different generations have different ways of relating. Some people are more psychologically oriented and can talk easily in psychological terms and communicate more intimately; others have a different mode of being and communicating. We have to meet people where they are at and not where we want them to be. It is difficult for parents to be different than they are; it is easier for us as younger adults to adapt to them than for them to adapt to us, within limits and reason.

It is sad when patterns in individuals and in families are so set that there does not seem to be the possibility of change. And so we need to try to change or weaken habits before they are too set, or else we'll have to learn to adapt in a creative way to an unchanging situation.

Recently returning from a walk I met a neighbor, an elderly woman, Mrs. Dupont, anxiously looking out on the pavement. I asked what was the matter and she told me that her car would not start and she needed to go shopping. She was looking for someone who was going to the supermarket. But nobody who was driving by understood her hand signals. I asked about her children and she told me that her son lived too far away. So I took her to the supermarket, as I seemed to be the only one aware and able to relieve her plight. Later on I learnt that Mrs. Dupont had a son living in the same village but that she had not talked to him for five years. Mrs. Dupont also had a good neighbor who used to help her but Mrs. Dupont had recently stopped talking to this friend ever since a carpenter who was repairing her friend's roof had blocked her garage and she had been unable to get out. Due to her pattern of high sensitivity to any slights, Mrs. Dupont's world is becoming more and more solitary. How can we as family members or friends go beyond such self-imposed exile and reach out in small ways to break through kindly and with understanding? It is important to see that if we close off, the further away we separate from a person the more difficult it will be later on to reconnect. We stop relating to the person in the present and keep relating to the image of the person we have in the past. It is not always easy to stay connected in the face of coldness, turning away, or criticisms. We need to cultivate courage, love, and stability to remain open.

Olga was asking me how she could practice love and equanimity toward her mother-law, Ingrid, who had a habit of alienating people and creating discord. I thought that she was already doing what was required, which was to be aware of the difficulty and to creatively deal with it while still loving and caring for Ingrid. Olga could see the suffering that this habit was creating for Ingrid. Her mother-in-law wanted to be loved and surrounded by her family and in fact the opposite was happening. One son had already moved away to another country. The only thing that Olga could do was to maintain contact and at the same time when this created difficulties with her children to protect them and explain to them Ingrid's patterns. It was important not to hide these patterns or excuse them as it was essential for the children to understand the situation and to learn that there are different kinds of people relating in different kinds of ways and to see what was destructive and what was constructive.

Gratitude

There exists a Buddhist text called *The Sutra about the Deep Kindness of Parents and the Difficulty of Repaying It.* This is the text that caused my teacher, Master Kusan, to cry whenever he thought of the sadness and concern of his mother when he left home. When he talked about it, it was so moving that I vividly saw the image of him leaving home and his mother crying on the doorstep. It is in this sutra that we find the ten types of kindness that a mother gives to a child:

The kindness of providing protection and care while the child is in the womb.
The kindness of bearing suffering during the birth.
The kindness of forgetting all the pain once the child has been born.

The kindness of eating the bitter herself and saving the
  sweet for the child.
The kindness of moving a child to a dry place and lying in
  the wet place herself.
The kindness of suckling the child at her breast and nour-
  ishing and bringing up the child.
The kindness of washing away the unclean.
The kindness of always thinking of the child when s/he is
  traveling far.
The kindness of deep care and devotion.
The kindness of ultimate compassion and sympathy.

These are practical points of reflection which make us realize how much we depended on our parents in our youth and
that they were kind to us in many different ways. However if
one or both of our parents are mentally ill or violent, they will
not be able to manifest all the kindnesses mentioned above.
One can be grateful for the ones they manifested, but the
larger family or friends need to protect and help the child and
compensate for the lack of stability and love.

So how can one be a good enough parent for a good enough
child? Raising children is not easy; they can be quite difficult,
often self-centered and strain parents' nerves. Parents need a
good dose of patient endurance to raise children. Again, the
middle way is what we should aspire to: to love our children
without stifling them and, while caring for their well being, to
bring discipline without blind regimentation. As any parent
can attest, parenting is the greatest practice one can find in
terms of love and equanimity—and it is a constant challenge
to make peace with impermanence and change.

MEDITATION INSTRUCTIONS
Loving-kindness Meditation

Sitting at home in the evening, reflect on all the beings you have related to during that day: partners, family members, friends, co-workers, strangers, and pets.

Beyond the content of any specific encounter, how did it feel to relate to someone else, to have a shared contact with another person?

Then focus on yourself, on your humanity, on the fact that you are alive and breathing. Try to wish yourself well, by repeating in silence within yourself these three sentences for a few minutes:

May I be healthy,
May I be happy,
May I be at peace.

Then bring to mind the people who live close to you and, looking beyond the ideas you might have of them, bring each in turn and wish them well by saying inwardly:

May you be healthy,
May you be happy,
May you be at peace.

Now open your heart to everything that is alive around where you live: trees, grasses, animals, people. Doing this, you open to their lives and potential, and wish them well too:

May you be healthy,
May you be happy,
May you be at peace.

Then expand your awareness to people you like and who have been of great help and support in your life and wish them well, repeating the three sentences for cultivating loving-kindness.

Then bring your attention to people you seem to feel indifferent and neutral to, people you meet in your daily life—a neighbor or the post-woman. Reach out to them and their life, hopes, and potential and wish them well also.

Then reflect on people you have difficulties with or that you do not like very much. First take the ones you have less problem with; as your heart becomes more stable and open, bring people of increasing difficulties. Wish them all well, being careful not to bring up and proliferate with the problems you have with them.

May you be healthy,
May you be happy,
May you be at peace.

Wish them well, looking beyond what you dislike about them and reach out to the person like yourself who is suffering and wants to be happy.

Finally you open your heart to the whole world:

May all beings be healthy,
May all being be happy,
May all being be at peace.

Try also to do this meditation when you are outside, walking in the park, sitting on a bench or in a bus, wishing well to each person you see and encounter.

9 Compassion

For this, friend, is the escape from cruelty, namely, the
liberation of the mind by compassion.

THE BUDDHA

Empathy

When a bird flew into a glass pane and stunned itself near a bonobo enclosure at a zoo, a female bonobo took care of it, first trying to throw it gently, then taking it to the top of a tree with its wings extended to make it fly and finally protecting it until it recovered and flew off. This is compassion; the ape is showing care and concern for some other smaller animal's suffering. In his book *Our Inner Ape*, Frans de Waal, a primatologist, tells of many other examples of such compassionate and caring attitude among the apes that he studied over more than twenty years. Frans de Waal's thesis is that like our close ancestors, the apes, we have an innate capacity for compassion. Studies have also shown that children just a little over one year old are concerned if people show signs of suffering and try to comfort them. Compassion arises naturally but we can also cultivate it intentionally to liberate our mind from cruelty as the Buddha suggested.

For compassion to arise, three qualities seem to be necessary. First (and obviously) we need to recognize the existence of the other person, secondly to empathize for his or her suffering, and thirdly to have time for and be available to that suffering. If we recognize our existence and the potential for happiness and suffering that comes with it, we also recognize others' existence and their potential for happiness and suffering. We cannot think someone else's thoughts; we cannot experience someone else's feelings. But we can imagine them and we can empathize with them. We can recognize that they are similar to our thoughts and feelings when we talk with them. From this we can deduce that they enjoy being at peace and happy, and they suffer when they are in pain just like us. In the recognition of the other there is also the recognition of the equality in the face of life.

When someone suffers, unless we have a very closed heart, we are moved by their suffering. Within our heart there is a natural response to suffering because we know and have experienced that suffering is painful. Moreover it is isolating. When we are in pain nobody can have our pain instead of us. This is why we feel all the more compassion for the person who is in pain. We cannot feel the pain but we can recognize the pain.

Compassion becomes active when we have time for and become available to the pain of the other. First we can be present and aware, empathizing with the person by listening and sharing a moment of that pain with him or her. Secondly we are prepared to do something about that pain, trying to alleviate it in any way that is at our disposal.

Four Types of Compassion

The Buddha suggested that there were three types of attitude with compassion and one without:

compassion only for oneself
compassion only for others
compassion equally for oneself and others
no compassion for self or others

It is essential to be compassionate to ourselves as we are also human beings with a potential for happiness and suffering. When we suffer it is important to take care of ourselves, to listen to our needs, to take a break, and to rest, but sometimes being mindfully aware of our suffering can become a pattern of self-obsession or self-victimization. If we are too concentrated on ourselves, we will grasp at the suffering and the suffering will become too prominent, taken out of any outer context. We will start to think and feel that we are the only one suffering or that our pains are the worst, not comparable or equal to anyone else's.

We have to be careful and find a middle way between being attentive to ourselves and becoming obsessed with ourselves. We could focus on suffering and this could open our heart and empathy. But if we were to turn any suffering into our own suffering, this could make us ignore other people's suffering because our own suffering would take precedence. I have an English friend who used to travel a lot and her mother is a worrier. Whenever there was an accident—a tragic train accident in Germany for example—the mother would be anxious that something happened to her daughter who was traveling in France. She did not feel compassion for the people who actually died and worried only for her daughter who was miles away from that accident.

What is our level of tolerance toward suffering? If our tolerance is low, it will be hard to measure the intensity of suffering because any suffering will be too much. If we think that suffering is unfair and that we should not ever have to experience it, this will lead us into conflict with reality. This can also make us manipulative as we try to avoid suffering at any cost and thus leads us to inflict suffering on others.

However, if you are only compassionate to others and never to yourself, it might bring resentment or exhaustion. Resentment will be created if the compassionate action you engage in is beyond your capacity to endure over a long period of time. Moreover bitterness might arise if you expect something in return for this compassion that you do not receive. Self-abnegation can be beautiful if it is not unreasonable. If you continuously give and never take care of yourself, then at some point you will be giving beyond your own health and strength. In some short burst it is wonderful to be self-abnegating and other-centered. But there are mental, emotional, and physical limits to your own being, generally it is not something that can be sustained over a long period of time.

Two years ago I was teaching a retreat and gave a talk about compassion. Afterward a young woman, Anna, came to me tearful and worried that she had not been compassionate enough with her husband. I asked her about the circumstances that led her to leave him. She told me that he was a drug addict, used all the money she earned and because of his drug habit had a lot of dealing with dangerous people. She finally left him because she felt it was becoming too dangerous and unsustainable. I inquired about how long she had loved him and supported him in this way, and she replied that it had been ten years. I suggested to her that she had been very compassionate and now it seemed that she needed to be as compassionate to herself as she had been to him.

We have to be careful not to fall into a pattern of being only compassionate to others as a means to feel valued and through which to gain or affirm our identity. The basis of our existence cannot rest solely on the needs others have of us. This is sometimes one of the difficulties facing mothers who have given so much to their children when the children grow up and leave home. The center of their existence seems to have gone and they feel a great emptiness in their lives. It is important that we care for others but it is also essential that we care for ourselves and let other people care for us.

The Buddha thought that the third type of person was the most balanced. It is healthy and sane to have as much compassion for oneself as for others. At the same time we have to accept that there is a spectrum of experienced and activated compassion. We are not trying to keep a fixed and equal measure all the time. There is no book in which compassion is added and totaled. According to circumstances sometimes we will have more compassion for others, then at other times we will need to have more compassion for ourselves, and at still other times we will be able to have compassion for ourselves and others equally. This does not depend on the state of our heart but on inner and outer circumstances—what is required and what we are able to contribute at that moment, be it physically, emotionally, or mentally.

A person who would have no compassion for either self or for other is quite rare—but there are circumstances that could lead to this. It could that one has learned to be tough and impermeable to suffering. It could be that one has no patience with compassion or suffering and see the world only in terms of winning or losing. It could be that one wants to exist beyond the restrictive elements of the heart, that one is trying to go beyond one's humanity in an abstract world of eternal peace. It could also be that one does not care for self or for others. Others would then be seen only as enemies, as strangers to be taken advantage of or to be eliminated as a nuisance and this could lead to cruelty. This is why the Buddha thought that compassion was an antidote to cruelty. In our own life what are the obstacles to compassion? What is it that stops us from being compassionate?

Obstacles to Compassion

Some of the main obstacles to compassion are busyness, stress, and fear. Busyness puts us in a strange state where we are feverishly focused on things. We are generally jumpy and agitated, ahead of ourselves, worried that we will not be able to do everything on time. We start to have tunnel vision; it is like we can see only a certain portion of reality and everything else becomes blurred and faint either side of that tunnel vision. In such a state, if we meet someone who is in difficulty, we cannot see him or her, we cannot respond as we are caught in the mental and emotional loop of "I'm busy, I don't have any time for this."

In order to respond compassionately you need to be stable and open; if you are too focused or too driven, there will not be any space for anything else. Yet also it is good to feel occupied, to have something to do—it makes you feel alive and active. Mindfulness can help you become aware when activities turn into something else, a driven busyness that reduced your potential for seeing others and responding to them.

If you are stressed, your whole body and mind become energized in a negative way and it is hard to rest or to sleep; thus it becomes difficult to function optimally as a human being. Your whole system is affected and often the unwholesome things you may do to relieve this stress will cut you off further from others even as it cuts you off from yourself. Turning to alcohol and drugs are two such unwholesome responses, but there are countless others.

Fear, as I mentioned in a previous chapter, will make you retreat into yourself in self-protection and will also make you oversensitive to the outside world. You will be constantly on alert for danger, which will preclude the door of compassion opening. Compassion asks of you to develop over time a courageous heart, which will enable you to move toward others in an easier manner. It is essential to go beyond your fears slowly in a wise manner.

Creative, Wise Compassion

Anyone can feel compassion if obstacles are not in the way, but it might not be necessarily *creative, wise compassion*. We have many habits, which will color our compassion in a restrictive way. One habit could be called "bartering," which means that we are compassionate but in the hope that we are going to get something in return and we feel short-changed or offended if there are no returns to our compassionate actions. This pattern can transmute into an "expecting" kind of compassion. This is when we, being compassionate, expect something, at least that the person will change for the better and of course that they will thank us for it. Often people do not change or change extremely slowly—and we might then experience "impatient" compassion, which would then lead us to think something like: "If people do not change, what is the point in helping them?"

Once I met a man, Richard, whose hobby was to help individuals that he happened to meet, who told me a wonderful story, which illustrates this "impatient" compassion. Once he saw a beggar, whose name he learned was Dan, in a terrible state on the street of Santa Monica. So he decided to help him. Dan had lost a leg, was a drug addict, and very dirty. Richard took him to a shelter where he could wash and helped him with official paperwork to get some financial support. However soon Dan went back to drugs and to the streets. Richard thought about giving up, but this made him feel bad. So he looked for Dan and decided to help him again. But Dan relapsed again into drugs and the streets and Richard gave up once more.

But he felt bad again. So he decided to go back to helping Dan but this time he decided he would do it differently and would not give up no matter what. So Richard found Dan again and told him that this time he would not give up and would be there for him through thick and thin. This unconditional commitment from Richard helped Dan see that his life was worth fighting for, that although he was disabled he still had potential and there could be hope for the future. He managed to turn his life around, worked with his addiction, and found a job and, eventually, a place to live.

Creative, wise compassion is freely given because there is a need and because it is in our power to do this or that. We do not need to be thanked for it. Of course people might be grateful and express their gratitude, but this is not a necessity for us. At times people just ask of us to be there for them. They do not want us to change them, they want to be seen and respected. Often what can be useful is to help transform outer conditions or remove obstacles so that they, themselves, are able to create and enrich their life.

Difficult People

Another habit that can restrict our compassion is being "picky and choosy." It is easy to be compassionate to people who resemble us, have similar opinions, whom we find likeable and easy to deal with. To be compassionate does not mean that we are not wise. We have compassion for the person but it does not mean that we condone the actions of the person if these actions are unethical or hurtful. But creative, wise compassion asks us to go beyond our boundaries and to open to everyone equally.

Creative, wise compassion makes you realize that people who are difficult are often unhappy. They have to live with themselves all the time, and this is often quite hard for them— you only meet them briefly or every so often. What is important is to try to engage them creatively when you meet them and to let go at once after you have left them or stopped talking to them. If you continue to argue with them in your thoughts, or argue with yourself inwardly after the meeting or the phone call, you are grasping at them, or at their or your own words, negatively and this will intensify and exaggerate the negativity and its importance.

In Zen, there is a traditional vow that says, "Sentient beings are numberless, I vow to save them all." This is related to having compassion for all beings. It does not mean that we are going to literally "save" every single being but rather that we intend to be open to all beings. To save them all can also be understood as to serve them all. This means that we do not intend to save people against their will but that as part of our practice we intend to be open and available to others' life and suffering.

Compassion and Equanimity

We have to be careful of not being overwhelmed by compassion. This is why the Buddha recommended to practice compassion and equanimity together. There is so much suffering and people in need all over the world that we can become paralyzed by the enormity of it. We need to be careful about our intake of news, be it from television or newspapers. It is important to be informed and to open our heart to the world but we have to do this wisely. Just to be a passive recipient to a lot of information can be counterproductive in that it makes us fearful, anxious, and overwhelmed. Often it is better to be less informed and be more active on the ground.

Every time we lead retreats in South Africa, we spend a few weeks at the Buddhist Retreat Center in Natal Province. This center is situated near a Zulu village where the cases of AIDS are numerous and the villagers are quite poor. First we helped the village schools. Becoming aware of the great number of young orphan families created by the death of both parents due to AIDS, we started to support one family of four young adults who had come to our attention. Then one day a friend suggested we visited a destitute family with young children with the view that we could help them too.

We went to a hut that was completely bare, save for a battered pot. There was an older woman who was only fifty but looked seventy and seemed totally depressed. She was the ailing grandmother of two young girls wearing rags and covered in scabies. The mother had run away and the father had died recently. Another daughter had died a week before and the grandmother had been unable to give food to the men who buried her daughter, as was the custom. Sitting in that hut I felt totally depressed myself, empathizing with the destitution of this family; knowing that there was no hope of the situation becoming better by the family's own means, as it had no means whatsoever. The whole family was reduced to begging in this already quite poor village. I was also struck by the realization that there must be many other families in a similar impossible situation all over South Africa, Africa, and the whole world.

So, of course, we started to support this family and bought them food, clothes, pots, and medicine. We enabled the children to go to school; they could not go until then because they did not have the proper clothes and could not pay the school fees. We found a way for them to get proper birth certificates so they could have official papers. When we received a photo of them next, they looked transformed: the grandmother looked only fifty and much happier, the little girls looked bright and energetic. Now the family could hope for a future because some people knew of their existence and cared for their well being. I am still worried about their long-term future and I am still saddened when I think of that hut, but I am happy that at least we could do something for them. Within me many feelings co-exist and my task is to acknowledge them without becoming overwhelmed and incapacitated by any of them.

We have to be careful that being aware of the suffering of the world does not activate our "Poor me! The world is hopeless and doomed and I feel so bad about it!" pattern, that it does not reinforce and exaggerate a certain sadness, which is lodged deep within ourselves. If we identify too much with the suffering of others and conflate it with our own suffering and then all the suffering in the world, it will quickly become unbearable. This is why we need to be wise and creative in our compassion so we can remain stable and responsive at the same time.

MEDITATION INSTRUCTIONS
Compassion and Equanimity

Lying down in bed, on the sofa, or on the grass, in a comfortable manner, be aware of the body resting there.

Opening your heart in compassion to your own pain, be it physical, mental, or emotional, without rejecting it or being caught by it, recite inwardly silently:

May I be free from pain,
May I be free from sorrow,
May I find peace.

After a few minutes, expand your heart and compassion to people you are at ease with and who are supportive and kind. Bring them to mind and feel for their pain in a stable and open manner and focus on these three sentences:

May you be free from pain,
May you be free from sorrow,
May you find peace.

Later on, open your heart and compassion to people you feel neutral toward. Recognize them, their life, and their suffering by repeating inwardly:

May you be free from pain,
May you be free from sorrow,
May you find peace.

After a while, expand your awareness to people you are connected with who are difficult. Recognize their pain and suffering and that they wish to be relieved from their suffering just like you do. Repeat the three sentences for them without becoming tense and negative:

May you be free from pain,
May you be free from sorrow,
May you find peace.

Then open your heart and compassion to the suffering of the whole world:

May all beings be free from pain,
May all beings be free from sorrow,
May all beings find peace.

At the end of the meditation, cultivate equanimity by focusing on these three sentences:

May I accept and know things as they are,
May I be balanced,
May I find equanimity.

10 Ethics

It is the duty of a bodhisattva to be always compassion-
ate and devoted toward others and to lead them all to
liberation by whatever means possible.

BRAHMA'S NET SUTRA

The Bodhisattva Path

A bodhisattva is a person who aspires to awakening not only for his or her own sake but also
for the sake of all beings. The *Brahma's Net*
Sutra presents the fifty-eight precepts that
will help the bodhisattva on his or her quest. Compassion is
seen as the source of the ethical attitude of the bodhisattva.
For example to engage in improper sexual behavior is seen
as one of the causes for compassion to disappear and that to
steal would not help one to make people happy and joyful.
In the precept asking one to care well for those who are sick,
it is suggested that to "fail to nurse and give assistance to
someone who is sick because of dislike or resentment would
be committing an offense." Another precept asks us to
"refrain from being angry and to treat well someone who asks
for forgiveness."

Buddhist ethics are based on compassion and the desire to
develop a cooperative, supportive, and harmonious society.
Compassion as a basis for ethics comes from the recognition

that suffering is equally painful for all. When I am hurt it is painful, just as when other people are hurt it is painful for them in the same way. The five basic ethical codes of conduct found in Buddhism are similar to basic ones found in other religions. They are:

Refrain from taking life.
Refrain from taking what is not given.
Refrain from improper sexual behavior.
Refrain from telling lies.
Refrain from taking intoxicants.

As soon as we are able to have empathy for ourselves, for life, for others, naturally we will try to be ethical and follow those basic precepts. It just makes sense to live that way as it leads to peace and harmony within ourselves and also within society.

Impulsivity

But what kind of habits would lead us to cause harm to others? Impulsiveness, anger, aggression, and self-centeredness are generally what do that. People who are impulsive and easily angry are more likely to harm people.

The principle that underlies all Buddhist precepts is non-harming. This principle invites us to reflect on the harm we cause. If we are sane human beings, we aspire not to cause pain to anyone. But impulsivity will make us hurt others in body, speech, and mind. This is why patience is such an important quality to cultivate. It is one of the ten perfections that can lead us to liberation. Patience is cultivated bodily when we sit in meditation and restrain the tendency to move and to act swiftly without consideration, also when we walk in meditation in a slow and steady manner. When we sit still or walk slowly in meditation, we are learning to be aware of all the impulses, feelings, and sensations that we experience in that moment. We become used to accepting our impulses, feelings, and sensations without identifying with them and thus let them pass through us without feeling that we have to act upon them immediately.

Over time this exercise can have a powerful effect on our impulsive nature. It does not eliminate it but it will channel it and reduce its intensity. When we are impulsive, we need to create stability and space so that we are not destabilized by our impulsive habits and act them out rashly.

This is often what prisoners who are doing meditation in prison find out. One prisoner, Bob, in one letter to a group that conducts meditation in prisons, wrote that when he stopped meditating for a few days, he saw that troubles rose up and his well-being diminished. In his own words: "I could feel the aggression and tension and lack of patience creeping back up onto my shoulders." The awareness that he had started to develop made him see clearly those destructive changes. He went quickly back to a regular meditation practice and was surprised by how soon he felt peaceful and at ease again.

It is for this reason that many successful meditation programs have been started in different prisons in different parts of the world. One well-known one is that of Kiran Bedi in Tihar jail in India. Now there is a meditation center in Tihar jail itself where thousand of inmates have done intensive ten-day meditation courses with great benefits.

Alone with Others

We are social beings. We are alone but inescapably linked to others in the world. Our societies have evolved not only through competition and self-interest but also through mutual support, care, and cooperation. Recently I read an article about water shortages in India. Since farmers have begun to use drilling rigs and electric pumps to get water from the water table to irrigate their fields, the water tables have fallen and the water is disappearing. The farmers who are conscious of this will say: "If I do not use this water, someone else will." This is one of the main recipes for the depletion of essential resources and destructive practices: "If I do not do it, someone else will, and so it might as well be me who does this and benefit from it even if it is defeating in the long run and the resource runs out."

In one Indian village one farmer decided to do what was done in ancient times—catch monsoon water runoff in tanks. But the farmer needed the help of other villagers to do this. Now their village is surrounded by greenery and people come far and wide to see what has been accomplished there, and a rainwater harvesting movement has started all over India.

According to the Buddha, unwholesome actions' destructive consequences come about through four causes: through desire, anger, ignorance, and fear. By ignorance he meant the fact that one does not see clearly that everything changes, and that everything including oneself arises out of conditions and does not exist independently. Ignorance is at the root of a lot of destructive consumption—as in the case of the water in India. Ignorance does not only blind us but also stops our creative potential from arising. Ignorance keeps us thinking only of the short-term benefits, hindering any reflections on the long-term consequences, which could lead one to find better long-term, constructive solutions.

Delusion and self-centeredness combined are powerful habits that reinforce each other. They do not make you stop and

LET GO

think about other ways to do things. Delusion and self-centeredness are often in action in daily life. At which point do you
feel concern and leave self-interest for general societal interest
in a greater good that will benefit not only yourself but also the
society at large? An understanding of causes and effects is an
essential element of a wise, co-operative, and ethical attitude.

Causes and Consequences

The *Sigalovada Sutra* is the Buddhist layperson code of conduct found in the Pali Discourses. In this text the Buddha
emphasized that cultivating an ethical attitude, which would
benefit oneself and others at the same time, comes from a
deep understanding of conditionality and of the fact that
actions always have effects.

For the Buddha, to live ethically was to be concerned not
only for your own spiritual well-being but also for your material well-being; material well-being which in turn would benefit not only your family but also the whole society. This is
what he stated in this verse:

> The wise man trained and disciplined
> Shines out like a beacon-fire.
> He gathers wealth just as the bee
> Gathers honey, and it grows
> Like an anthill higher yet.
> With wealth so gained the layman can
> Devote it to his people's good.
> He should divide his wealth in four.
> One part he may enjoy at will,
> Two parts he should put to work,
> The fourth part he should set aside
> As reserve in times of need.

An ethical attitude entails working on negative habits, which lead us to cause harm to others, but also to cultivate positive actions, which will enable us to develop a harmonious and cooperative society. This is why in the *Sigalovada Sutra* the Buddha talks at length about supportive relationships, be it within a family, a clan, among friends, between teacher and students, between employers and employees. The Buddha recommended being gentle but also intelligent, generous as well as impartial, hospitable, and energetic at the same time.

Modern Ethics

Ethics are not just rules and regulations that people must follow because they are forced to in fear of punishment or ostracism from society. Rather, ethical precepts are points of reflection, which help us to look at patterns, habits, and attitudes that are destructive to ourselves, others, and the world, so that we can dissolve or at least weaken these destructive habits.

From a Buddhist point of view, ethics would be about cultivating self-respect and consideration for others in body, speech, and mind. An ethical attitude would make us look at our motivation, at our actions; their results may be visible or invisible. This is a training in awareness and wisdom.

In exploring these topics with students, one of the main themes that emerges is a need for global and ecological awareness. People feel that because certain resources are limited, each of us has a responsibility of looking at what we produce and consume and how this could have a destructive impact on the whole planet. Gandhi, in his time, asked people to consider causing the least harm within their possibilities. Each human being has to survive but not selfishly at the expense of others or a whole planet. We are individuals, responsible for our own actions. We cannot impute them to others. In terms of the protection and sustainability of the environment, we have to look at our situation and circumstances and see what we can do. I buy fresh local produce from a weekly country market but not everyone has a market nearby. An ethical attitude must be adapted to our circumstances and to what makes sense in our situation.

Ethical Speech

Speaking ethically, wisely, and constructively is very important. Words can be a powerful weapon of aggression or manipulation, but can also cause harm simply when used carelessly.

People spend a fair amount of time gossiping, criticizing, backstabbing, colluding, and sniggering. Although every conversation does not, of course, have to be about the meaning of life or the origin of the universe, it is important to bring an ethical attitude to our speech and to see when it turns destructive and hurtful in direct or indirect ways. Awareness is the key: What do I say? How do I say it? To whom do I say it? What is my aim in saying it?

Gossiping is part of human life but when it becomes malicious, it can create great harm, especially when it creates collusion and is used to shore up one's position. Notice when you have a problem with someone how you enlist your friends to reinforce your position, or when a group of people has difficulties with another group of people how each will spend a lot of time repeating endlessly among themselves the arguments why they are right and others are wrong. This will not lead to peace and harmony or to a creative solution to the problem.

As an exercise, try for a week to not speak about someone else if he or she is not present. You will discover that your conversation will be reduced dramatically! Your mind will also be calmer, since you will diminish the time you spend endlessly thinking critically about other people.

To be ethical is to be aware and to hold dear certain values like harmlessness, generosity, wisdom, and compassion and to make an effort for these values to be lived and activated in our daily life, not only within ourselves but also within our social relationships.

MEDITATION INSTRUCTIONS
Reflections for an Ethical Life

What do you do for your mind? What does your mind do for you?

Your mind is precious and allows you to be conscious and wise. It would be helpful to respect its work and what it does for you. What can you do to contribute to that?

What do you do for your body? What does your body do for you?

Your body sustains you and enables you to exist. What can you do to contribute to its health and sustaining?

What do you do for your family? What does your family do for you?

If your family is loving and supportive, can you participate in cultivating and developing this love and support?

What do you do for your friends? What do your friends do for you?

If your friends are there for you, how can you be there for them?

What do you do for your society? What does your society do for you?

If you are born in a relatively stable and open society, how can you help this society in a creative way?

What do you do for the world? What does the world do for you?

The world provides you with culture and connection. What can you do to sustain culture and develop more connection?

What do you do for the earth? What does the earth do for you?

You depend on the earth for your life. How can you contribute to the life and health of the earth?

11 A Creative Path

The old year goes
Casting its sorrows on the coming year
But spring brings fresh color to things;
The mountain flowers laugh at the verdant waters;
Bees and butterflies are happiness itself
And birds and fishes are utterly lovable;
Friends came to see me—the joy of them
So lingered that from evening to dawn
I could not sleep.

HANSHAN (CHINESE POET, TANG DYNASTY)

Daily Life

Our life is spent in villages, towns, or big cities, often far away from the delights of nature. We might have the opportunity to go on meditation retreats in the countryside for a weekend, a week, or a month but our life is working, relating, waiting in line, shopping in the supermarket, and so on. On a meditation retreat, the challenge is to accept the moment as it is and follow the schedule; in daily life the challenge is not to become overwhelmed and destabilized by the tumult of impressions, interactions, information, opinions, and emotions that swirl in and around us. If we can find stability and clarity in the multi-dimensionality of our life, then a creative path can open for us—a new way of looking and seeing.

In the Zen tradition, there is a series of images called the "Ten Oxherding Pictures," which depict the various stages on the meditative path. These images can be a good map to describe the process involved in dealing creatively with destructive habits in daily life. The theme of the images is the search for peace, harmony, and awakening. The images themselves tell the story of a young boy, an oxherder, who is looking for his ox.

Searching for the Ox

The first picture represents the young boy lost in nature, among trees and rivers, and looking frantically for his ox. This image shows the stage wherein we do not realize that we are caught in our destructive habits. We are like a person blindfolded walking here and there bumping into the furniture and falling into holes. We are in pain and are causing pain to others. We are strangely unsatisfied but don't know what the problem is. We may feel uncomfortable in our own skin. At this stage, we often think that the problem comes from outside—and we look outside for a solution, to make everything smoother and easier.

Here, we may turn to sex and relationships to fill a certain void, intoxicants to anesthetize the pain, sport and exercise to channel our energy, entertainment to distract us, work for a sense of accomplishment, material things to give us comfort. But any of these things or all of them together never satisfy us entirely. They do not resolve our basic problems of suffering, lack, or conflicts. They do not lead to peace.

Seeing the Footprints

The second picture shows the ox-herder seeing footprints. This is the stage wherein we start to have an inkling that the problems are not all coming from the outside but may have to do with ourselves and the way we behave and use our minds. We are beginning to be less blinded by our own habits. We start to recognize that what we think is not necessarily true. Because we think something or want something in a certain way does not mean that it will happen the way we want it to happen. We have to leave behind a certain immature state, which makes us assume that everything revolves around us. We start to be more organically in life and less abstractly. We see conditions, causes, and consequences. We start to aspire to certain values for ourselves and also for our society.

In terms of meditation, this is the stage wherein we encounter traces of spirituality, which touches us. We see it as a missing dimension in our life. Personally I could see that I was stuck in habits of thinking and feeling and that I could not transform them just by willing it.

Seeing the Ox

In the third image the young boy intermittently sees the back of the ox among the foliage. Finally he has seen the ox and knows that it exists and is close at hand. This is the time when we start to see very clearly what the problem is and when we catch a glimpse of the "solution." We see that difficult mental, physical, and emotional habits arise upon certain conditions. Sometimes they are there, sometimes not. Sometimes we are peaceful and happy and sometimes we get into terrible states when we do not recognize ourselves.

In terms of meditation, this is when you are searching for a method, a way that you can use. It is essential that whatever method you choose corresponds to what you aspire to, that it makes sense, that you can do it relatively easily, that it does not go against your basic values of ethics, wisdom, compassion, and non-harming. It is important that the path that you embark upon is open and non-dogmatic (or at least not too dogmatic), that you do not feel a prisoner in the group, that you are able to keep your own judgment and are not asked to abdicate it, that you are not disempowered, that the method that you use helps you to be more stable and open, and finally that it is not too expensive.

Catching the Ox

The fourth picture is, in my opinion, the most powerful one of the whole series. The ox-herder has managed to catch the ox with a rope but the ox does not want to be caught. It jumps and pulls all over the place. The boy has to hold on to the rope tightly in order to stand his ground. This represents the stage when you decide to do something about your habits. You will not give in anymore. You will restrain yourself and you decide not to become angry, jealous, or anxious.

But you realize that just thinking about not following your old harmful habits is not sufficient. You have to develop your own creative power to counteract the power of habits, which have themselves been cultivated for a long time. So it is a struggle, the habits move you one way, but you begin to be able to resist—and at this stage you may feel like you become a battleground. Giving in is alluring and may be remembered as being so much easier, but you know the painful consequences of falling into these behaviors. So you stand firm in your intention and you resist with all your might. At this stage, meditation is a tool that begins to help you transform your relationship to your own patterns by stabilizing you and making you see them more clearly.

In terms of meditation, this is the moment when, having found a meditative path, we really do it ourselves. We sit still, try to concentrate and inquire, and we find that this is very difficult to do. As soon as we try to focus, our mind wanders away. We cannot concentrate for more than a few seconds at a time. If we are not lost in thoughts, we start to feel dull and sleepy. If we do not feel slothful, we have pains in the knee or the back. It seems an impossible task, just to sit still and be aware of the moment as it is. However if we stand firm, keep on trying, and manage to sit still and meditate, we can start to feel the effect of that effort and dedication. Meditation nurtures our whole being. We feel quieter and start to see more clearly the mechanism of our painful habits.

Tending the Ox

In the fifth picture the boy still holds the rope, but loosely, and he and the ox are walking alongside each other. There is no tension anymore. We can look at the habits directly and know them for what they are. We do not exaggerate them anymore. They exist and we recognize that we have certain tendencies and particularities, which interact with outer conditions. We can accept this and the conditions we encounter. That deep acceptance and knowledge make the habits more ordinary and possible to deal with. This is the stage where the power of the habits has diminished and we can engage with them in an ordinary manner. This is not a heroic combat anymore.

These are still the early days though, so you have to be careful. This is why the ox-herder is still holding the rope. Your power is not totally firm yet. You might easily regress, so you must remain attentive and ready to respond swiftly and yank the ox if suddenly it jumped away and tried to run again. This is when you are tempted by old habits suddenly after a calm period. With creative awareness you are able to see through the inclination and prevent the habit from taking hold. You have tools that you can use: patience, stability, generosity, endurance, and skillfulness. Instead of falling into the old patterns, you know something else is possible and so you do that something else.

In terms of meditation, we have become familiar with the technique. The mind is more malleable, the body is more comfortable and the heart is starting to open. Meditation is not a strange and foreign activity anymore. We can do it regularly at home or informally in daily life. It becomes part of the fabric of our life. At times, we might encounter some obstacles—some restlessness or fatigue—but we deal with them skillfully as they come. They do not overwhelm us because our faith and our ability have become more settled.

Riding the Ox Back Home

The sixth picture is an image of joy and ease. The boy is sitting astride the ox playing the flute. This shows that when you break free from your patterns, you start to be more joyful and creative. At this stage you realize that being stuck in patterns not only caused you suffering but also impeded your joy and your creativity. By breaking free from the habits that limited you, a whole world of possibilities opens up for you.

You can start to follow your creative inclination. If you have a garden, you might begin to see it as an arena for playing with color and texture. Cooking can become a joy. You can still cook simply but with interesting ingredients and different ways of preparing them. You might discover tastes, color, and texture.

You may experiment with spices, condiments, and presentation. Placing the food on the plate can become an artistic endeavor. You feel the healthy desire to create something out of nothing, just for the joy of creating for its own sake, not to exhibit or compete but to express yourself with whatever material you feel affinity with, be it words, paint, wood, stone, or cloth. By letting go of your habits your creative potential is released.

Whenever my seven-year-old niece comes to spend some time with us, we draw together on the kitchen table, each with her own blank piece of paper. We use the same multicolored pens. I draw shapes and fill them with color, each color calling out for the next color. My niece draws houses, people, flowers, and animals. We check and admire each other's drawing as we go along. It is a congenial and creative time together. We are not trying to prove anything to each other. We just enjoy drawing together, each of us using her own ability and sense of color and shape.

In the sixth stage, meditation becomes easier. There is a flow of awareness and intention. There is less grasping, so thoughts, sensations, and feelings come and go without sticking. There is a deep stability but also a great lightness in your whole being. You do not have to think about meditating, it happens by itself. You take yourself less seriously; you see more humor in the life that presents itself to you. Others can also share and benefit from your lightness and ease.

Forgetting the Ox, the Ox-herder Rests Alone

In the seventh picture, the ox has disappeared and the boy sits at home quietly in the evening watching the moon. Once free of the habits that create and intensify our suffering, our life becomes ordinary in a beautiful way. Each moment reveals to us its richness and its intricacies. By letting go of fears and worries, we are more present and can live more fully.

We lose such fear as being bored or not being special. We revel in the ordinariness of hearing, seeing, smelling, tasting, thinking, and being. We breathe and it is a wonder that we are able to do that. We enjoy sitting quietly without anything to do. We recognize the beauty of being alive at all—at being able to sit in the evening and appreciate the radiance of the moon.

In terms of meditative practice, at this point we see that there is no separation between meditation and our life. Every act can be a meditative act. We can bring meditative awareness to whatever we do—working, resting, listening, or communicating. As my Korean teacher used to say: "Even when we go to the toilet we meditate." Being creatively aware is the natural thing to do. We do not have to force ourselves to be aware. It happens by itself and this enriches our life and our relationships.

The Ox and the Ox-herder are Both Forgotten

In the eighth picture there is just an empty circle: both boy and ox have disappeared. Once the roots of the habits have dissolved, your life is simplified. Habits brought complication to your life. Previously, any small incident or encounter could be transformed into a huge difficulty that would last days. Previously everything was so terribly important. Now what used to be a trigger to your painful habits has no place to activate. It is like a river going into the sea—there are no special ripples, just a continuity of water. In the same way, in a life free of habits, there is a continuity of actions and life flowing into each other, fuelled by creative responses. The actions and responses come from a spacious, stable, and open place and return to a spacious, stable, and open place. Nothing is disturbed.

You have realized that there is no place for the habits to exist and no substance to the habits. There are just ephemeral phenomena. When the grasping goes, there is no place to stick. This is what is remarkable: the habits seemed so strong and all-powerful, but actually they were not. They have been defused. At this stage you see and experience that you are not as fixed, limited, and as solid as you thought that you were. There is more fluidity, flexibility, and possibility of movement than you thought. Your life becomes a narrative story that you can create; your own gaze or the gaze of others does not fix you.

Recently I read *White on Black* written by Ruben Gallego. It is his life story told in vignettes. It is sad, humbling, and inspiring. He was born with cerebral palsy, unable to walk and abandoned in an orphanage. His Spanish mother had been told that he had died. His conditions were horrendous. People who "cared" for him told him often that he was useless, a burden on society and would be better off dead.

But he was extremely intelligent and creative, and he survived. His survival as an intact, kind, creative, and humorous human being in that destructive environment is a miracle, entirely due to his power of awareness and observation. What saved him was that he did not identify with his physical limitations nor with the diminished image others had of him. He did not thwart his creative potential. This potential was within him, sustained him, and helped him to blossom even amid his ordeals.

Returning to the Original Place

The ninth picture represents nature; it is filled with trees and flowers. It is similar to the first picture but there is no agitation or tension. Now that the power of the patterns and habitual reactions are gone, we are less self-centered and agitated so we can encounter nature in a different way and thus feel our deep connections to it. Awareness of nature enables us to reconnect to the microcosm—a tiny insect, some drops of dew on a petal—and the macrocosm—the earth, the stars—at the same time. Seeing nature makes us experience our own nature. Connecting with nature has the power of healing our habitual feelings of isolation and separateness, and enables us to feel alive with the whole of life.

The resources and beauty of nature can nurture us if we recognize them and let them touch us. As Kojisei wrote: "The song of birds, the voices of insects, are all means of conveying truth to the mind; in flowers and grasses we see messages of the way. The scholar, pure and clear of mind, serene and open of heart, should find in everything what nourishes him." By abstracting ourselves from nature, we lose out. When we listen to the song of the birds and the voices of insects, we come back to the present, to this experience, to this moment. We become part of life and are nourished by it. The smallest part of nature can have a great teaching for us if we notice it and meet it as it manifests.

Entering the Marketplace with Helping Hands

In the last picture, the young boy reappears and is accompanied by a bare-footed, pot-bellied man bearing gifts. This image shows us that once we break free of habits, our heart opens and we become more available to others. When we are caught in painful habits, it is hard to see others clearly and compassionately. We are too afraid, anxious, or self-centered. When we awaken from the grip of the destructive patterns, we see and are available for others in a creative and skillful way.

Meditation has not made us become automatons; on the

contrary it has revealed new parts of ourselves, which can be developed and expressed creatively for the benefit of the people we encounter. In my various travels I have been struck by how people, once they have gone beyond the limits of their self-involvement, can become involved with others in such creative and manifold ways. Once I met a Buddhist nun in the South of Taiwan, in a massive Buddhist complex comprising orphanages, colleges, and temples—who was the resident engineer nun and the supervisor for the construction work. She had became a nun to learn Buddhism and to practice the Dharma, but now she felt like the whole world was a big family and she wanted to serve it usefully.

What does it mean not to be selfish? What does it mean to have compassion and understanding for other people? Each of us can find our own way to meet and benefit others. We do not need to copy others; we just have to open to our own capacities, the world we inhabit and the people we encounter.

A Spiraling Process

When we look at these ten stages, we have to be careful not to think of them as being linear and happening gradually, one after the other, over a lifetime. All the ten stages can happen in a single day! In reality, though, the process is more like a spiral. We go around and up with each cycle. We may find ourselves back in earlier stages but in a different way and circumstance. We must deepen our experience and understanding of each stage as we revisit them. We will still have traces of habits to see and dissolve. Yet we will discover more ways to develop stability and openness. My teacher, Master Kusan, had three different major awakenings, and each time he continued to practice even more. There is no end to the development of wisdom, compassion, and creativity. The creative path is endless. It is not the end that is important but the walking of the path itself, the willingness to work with ourselves and with others, the faith we have in the fact that we can walk and practice this path and benefit from its fruits.

MEDITATION INSTRUCTIONS
Creativity

What are the things that might help you to become creative? Here are a few ways to find out:

First, find the time to do nothing,

No agenda, no expectations, no plans.

Then find some tools: pens, oils, instruments, colored threads, etc. . . .

Touching them and knowing them, open to the moment.

Pay close attention to light, colors, shapes, sounds, movements.

What do they inspire in you?

Allow yourself to be enlightened by all things.

Just look, just listen.

Try to see the world in a new way,

Recovering a sense of wonder,

Discovering the beauty of the ordinary.

Art is in the doing,

Open yourself to an imaginative gesture,

Create something out of nothing:

Draw shapes, design a framework, tap a drum, or write some words.

Try to suspend critical judgment,

Let your creative urges manifest,

Can you create something that did not exist before?

Afterword

The golden orioles fly through the sky,
They leave no prints.
The reed's shadows sweep the water,
There is no ripple.

Acknowledgments

Deep gratitude to all the people who have come on our retreats, who have managed and organized them. Great thanks to all the team at Wisdom who made this book possible. I am indebted to Charlie Blacklock, John Teasdale and Prof. Schwartz for their invaluable help. I appreciated Dorrit Wagner's comments on some of the chapters. I was sustained during the writing process by my husband, Stephen's unfailing good humor, patience and love.

Bibliography

Batchelor, Martine. *The Path of Compassion*. Walnut Creek, CA: Altamira Press, 2004.

Beck, Aaron T. *Reflections on My Public Dialog with the Dalai Lama*. Goteborg, 13 June 2005, www.beckinstitute.org.

Bryson, Bill. *A Short History of Everything*. London: Black Swan Books, 2004.

Cohen, Darlene. *Finding a Joyful Life in the Heart of Pain*. Boston: Shambhala, 2000.

Galland, China. "The Formless Form: Buddhism and the Community of Recovery." in *Being Bodies*, edited by Leonore Friedman and Susan Moon, 185–96. Boston: Shambhala, 1997.

Gallego, Ruben. *White on Black*. Translated by Marian Schwartz. New York: Harcourt, 2006.

Graves, Theodore D. *Studies in Behavioral Anthropology*. Vols. 1 and 2. Las Vegas, NV: Marion Street Publishing, 2002.

Gregson, David and Jay S. Efran. *The Tao of Sobriety*. New York: Thomas Dunne Books, 2002.

Hobson, Peter, trans. *Poems of Hanshan*. Walnut Creek, CA: Altamira Press, 2003.

Huxter, Malcolm. *Mindfulness and a Path of Understanding: A Workbook for the Release from Cycles of Stress, Anxiety and Depression*, (2006—unpublished)

BIBLIOGRAPHY

Kabat-Zinn, Jon. *Full Catastrophe Living.* New York: Delta, 1990.

Kiedis, Anthony. *Scar Tissue.* New York: Hyperion, 2005.

Levine, Noah. *Dharma Punx.* San Francisco: HarperSanFrancisco, 2003.

Nyanaponika Thera and Bhikkhu Bodhi, eds. and trans. *Numerical Discourses of the Buddha.* Walnut Creek, CA: Altamira Press, 1999.

Peabody, Susan. *Addiction to Love.* Berkeley, CA: Celestial Arts, 1994.

Prison Phoenix Trust Newsletter, www.prisonphoenixtrust.org.uk

Pearce, Fred. "Earth: The Parched Planet." *New Scientist,* February 25, 2006.

S., Laura. *12 Steps on Buddha's Path: Bill, Buddha and We.* Boston: Wisdom Publications, 2006.

Schwartz, Jeffrey M. and Sharon Begley. *The Mind and the Brain.* New York: Regan Books, 2002.

Schwartz, Jeffrey M. and Beverly Beyette. *Brain Lock.* New York. Regan Books, 1997.

Segal, Zindel V., J. Mark G. Williams, and John D. Teasdale. *Mindfulness-Based Cognitive Therapy for Depression.* New York: The Guilford Press, 2002.

Sigalovada Sutra, in *The Long Discourses of the Buddha,* translated by Maurice Walshe. Boston: Wisdom Publications, 1987.

Solomon, Andrew. *The Noonday Demon.* New York: Scribner, 2001.

The Sutra about the Deep Kindness of Parents and the Difficulty of Repaying It, in "Mahayana Buddhist Sutras in English." at www4.bayarea.net/~mtlee/

Upchurch, Carl. *Convicted in the Womb.* New York: Bantam, 1997.

Valleur, Mark and Jean-Claude Matysiak. *Les Nouvelles Formes d'Addiction.* Paris: Edition Flammarion, 2004.

De Waal, Frans. *Our Inner Ape.* London: Granta Publications, 2005.

Wright, Robert. *Nonzero: The Logic of Human Destiny.* New York: Pantheon, 2000.

Index

About Wisdom Publications

Wisdom Publications, a nonprofit publisher, is dedicated to making available authentic works relating to Buddhism for the benefit of all. We publish books by ancient and modern masters in all traditions of Buddhism, translations of important texts, and original scholarship. Additionally, we offer books that explore East-West themes unfolding as traditional Buddhism encounters our modern culture in all its aspects. Our titles are published with the appreciation of Buddhism as a living philosophy, and with the special commitment to preserve and transmit important works from Buddhism's many traditions.

To learn more about Wisdom, or to browse books online, visit our website at www.wisdompubs.org.

You may request a copy of our catalog online or by writing to this address:

Wisdom Publications
199 Elm Street
Somerville, Massachusetts 02144 USA
Telephone: 617-776-7416
Fax: 617-776-7841
Email: info@wisdompubs.org
www.wisdompubs.org

The Wisdom Trust

As a nonprofit publisher, Wisdom is dedicated to the publication of Dharma books for the benefit of all sentient beings and dependent upon the kindness and generosity of sponsors in order to do so. If you would like to make a donation to Wisdom, you may do so through our website or our Somerville office. If you would like to help sponsor the publication of a book, please write or email us at the address above.

Thank you.

Wisdom is a nonprofit, charitable 501(c)(3) organization affiliated with the Foundation for the Preservation of the Mahayana Tradition (FPMT).

Meditation for Life
Martine Batchelor
Photographs by Stephen Batchelor
168 pages, ISBN 0-86171-320-8, $22.95

"Among today's steady stream of new books on Buddhist meditation, most are easy to ignore. This one isn't. It offers simple, concrete instructions in meditation and the photographs are delicious eye candy."—Psychology Today

"This is truly a lovely work—graceful, elegant, clear, helpful, and wise. *Meditation for Life* demystifies meditation while making it available to all who need it. A treasure."—Mark Epstein, author of *Thoughts without a Thinker*

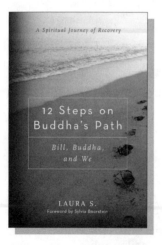

12 Steps on Buddha's Path
Bill, Buddha, and We
Laura S
Foreword by Sylvia Boorstein
160 pages, ISBN 086171-281-1, $12.95

An inspiring firsthand account of what happens when life seems hopeless, and the miracle of finding out that it's anything but.

"This book is an excellent introduction to 12-Step and Buddhist principles, and an insightful synthesis of the two traditions. Anyone seeking to understand recovery from a Buddhist perspective will find it to be a trustworthy and illuminating guide."—Kevin Griffin, author of *One Breath at a Time: Buddhism and the Twelve Steps*